DISGUISED UNEMPLOYMENT IN
AN UNDERDEVELOPED ECONOMY

Disguised Unemployment in an Underdeveloped Economy

ITS NATURE AND MEASUREMENT

J. S. UPPAL

Professor of Economics
State University of New York
Albany

ASIA PUBLISHING HOUSE

NEW YORK

ISBN 0. 210. 22269.7

PRINTED IN INDIA

BY THE A. J. PRINTERS, BAHADUR SHAH ZAFAR MARG, NEW DELHI, AND PUBLISHED BY P. S. JAYASINGHE, ASIA PUBLISHING HOUSE, NEW YORK.

PREFACE

IN THE recent literature on economic development, increasing attention has been devoted to the phenomenon of disguised unemployment. Confusion exists in the literature because the same terminology has been applied to different and often inconsistent situations, and conclusions based on measuring a particular type of disguised unemployment have been drawn as if they were valid for the phenomenon in general.

The study is divided into two parts. The first part is devoted to the theory of disguised unemployment. In Chapter One, the theoretical framework distinguishing the various causes of disguised unemployment is formulated, and the relevant literature is surveyed, with special reference to the social and economic conditions in the rural sector of the underdeveloped countries. Chapter Two is devoted exclusively to the analysis of disguised unemployment due to an excess aggregate labour supply relative to the aggregate supplies of cooperating factors, because this is believed to be the primary cause of unemployment in many agrarian societies. In Chapter Three, we examine some models of a dual economy, with a family firm sector and a hired labour sector, relating disguised unemployment to the process of economic development. Some social and cultural factors affecting the removal of surplus farm labour for utilization elsewhere are also noted.

Second part of the study is concerned with the measurement of disguised unemployment. Chapter Four consists of a survey of attempts that have been made to measure the extent of disguised unemployment in various parts of the world. Chapter Five describes a simple technique of measuring the extent of disguised unemployment by comparing the labour/land and land/output ratios for different sizes of holdings, after taking into account the effect of "other factors," such as the technique of cultivation, irrigation, and capital investments. This technique is applied to data published by the Government of India in connection with its Farm Management Studies.

The study was begun at the suggestion of Professor Martin Bronfenbrenner, now at the Duke University, U.S.A. to whom the writer owes a great debt for guiding this study, and giving valuable counsel at all stages. The writer also wishes to express his sincere gratitude to Professor Edward Coen for his helpful advice and kind support in completing the study. The author, of course, holds himself alone responsible for any shortcomings the study may suffer from.

The author is deeply grateful to Professors Leonid Hurwicz and David Cooperman for their kindness and constant encouragement. The research was supported by the John Cowles Foundation Fellowship for which the author wishes to express his gratitude.

Part one of the study was circulated by the Economics and Agricultural Development Institute, Michigan State University, East Lansing, Michigan, U.S.A., as a Research Monograph. The author expresses his gratitude to the Editors for the permission to adapt and reprint his articles published in the following journals : *The Oxford Economic Papers; The Canadian Journal of Economics and Political Science* and *Economia Internazionale*.

J. S. UPPAL

State University of New York
Albany, New York 1973

CONTENTS

CHAPTER ONE

NATURE OF DISGUISED UNEMPLOYMENT

A. THEORETICAL FRAMEWORK

IN THIS chapter we shall survey the literature which is concerned primarily with the theoretical aspects of disguised unemployment. The many interpretations given to the concept of disguised unemployment can be broadly classified by cause, as shown in the table on the following page which focuses attention on the causes of unemployment.

To explain why this unemployment is disguised rather than overt, we need to look into the institutional arrangements for supporting the unemployed. Because of the inadequacy of State aid for the unemployed, they are supported by their families. Since most families are also family firms which either do not hire wage labour, or hire only at times of peak activity, the unemployed members of the family are required to share the work burden of the family firm, even though they have not been hired on a strictly commercial basis. This disguise can characterize all the types of unemployment tabulated on the following page. A brief explanation of the various types of disguised unemployment is in order.

1 DISGUISED UNEMPLOYMENT DUE TO A DEFICIENCY OF AGGREGATE DEMAND

Because of a deficiency of effective demand during the down swing of the business cycle, coupled with a downward inflexibility of the wage rate in the short run, a number of hired workers are rendered unemployed. In the absence of unemployment benefits, the unemployed engage themselves in less productive work. They may peddle cigarettes or shine shoes or return to the family farm or shop. These workers, though technically at work, have been characterized as disguised unemployed, since their present jobs do not fully utilize their skills. This problem is primarily macroeconomic and can be remedied through appropriate fiscal and monetary policies. With the revival of effective demand, the workers return to their more productive jobs. Disguised unemployment in this sense is not of great quantitative relevance for underdeveloped countries. In these economies, the level of effective demand cannot be usually raised without inflation.

TABLE 1

CAUSES OF DISGUISED UNEMPLOYMENT

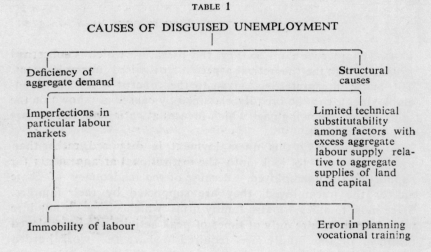

Deficiency of aggregate demand

Structural causes

Imperfections in particular labour markets

Limited technical substitutability among factors with excess aggregate labour supply relative to aggregate supplies of land and capital

Immobility of labour

Error in planning vocational training

2 DISGUISED UNEMPLOYMENT DUE TO STRUCTURAL CAUSES

Assuming an adequate level of aggregate demand, disguised unemployment can still arise from structural deficiencies. A convenient way of defining and classifying these deficiencies is to distinguish between the following two problems:

(a) The aggregate supply of labour is not excessive (in a sense to be defined later) relative to the aggregate supplies of land and capital, and yet, as a result of frictions in the adjustment process, excess supplies of labour might persist in particular labour markets, or the marginal value product of a particular type of labour might not be equalized in all the firms which employ that type of labour.

(b) Conversely, the aggregate labour supply might be so great, relative to the aggregate supplies of land and capital, that even in the absence of adjustment frictions, the final equilibrium could not yield full employment at any reasonable wage rate.

3 IMPERFECTIONS IN PARTICULAR LABOUR MARKETS

(*i*) If homogeneous labour inputs lack geographical mobility, their marginal value product would differ in different regions. This condition has been referred to as disguised unemployment.

(*ii*) Factors which reduce workers' mobility between alternative occupations would increase inequalities between the marginal value products in those occupations.

(*iii*) Over-optimistic forecast of the demands for particular skills. Downward inflexibility of wage rates bars entry into the corresponding occupations, and they are compelled to enter other occupations yielding a lower marginal value product. The term "latent disguised unemployment" has been employed in this connection.

These defects in the adjustment mechanism in particular labour markets are certainly not peculiar to underdeveloped economies, though they may be more pronounced than in the advanced economies.

4 EXCESS AGGREGATE LABOUR SUPPLY RELATIVE TO COOPERATING INPUTS

In most underdeveloped economies, labour abundance, capital and land shortage describe the factor endowment position. If the production function has limited opportunities for factor substitution, then, beyond a certain point, employment of more labour may not add to the total output. Even a hypothetical, perfectly working and competitive market mechanism does not yield a full employment solution to this set of initial conditions. The rational employer will not reduce the real wage rate below the point where a further fall in the real wage lowers the average productivity of his labour force by an amount exceeding the decline in the real wage.

Therefore, all workers with marginal products below this minimum wage rate would be overtly unemployed. The perfectly competitive market mechanism has no solution for them except to vanish from the market. Fortunately, institutions like the joint family system, where the family shares its food and work with needy relatives, permit these workers to be supported. It is this last type of disguised unemployment which most distinguishes unemployment in underdeveloped countries from unemployment in advanced countries.

In the remainder of this chapter, we will subject each of the above categories of disguised unemployment to a more detailed examination.

B.   DISGUISED UNEMPLOYMENT DUE TO DEFICIENCY OF AGGREGATE DEMAND

The author of the term "disguised unemployment," Mrs. Joan Robinson (207) defined it as, "the adoption of inferior jobs by the workers laid off from their normal jobs due to lack of effective demand during depression." She uses this concept in the context of Keynes' *General Theory of Employment, Interest and Money*. Broadly speaking, Keynes argued that unemployment is caused by a lack of effective demand and can be removed through appropriate fiscal and monetary policies without a reduction in money wages. Elaborating on this view, Mrs. Robinson remarked:

> In a society in which there is no regular system of unemployment benefit and in which poor relief is either non-existent or "less eligible" than almost any alternative short of suicide, a man who is thrown out of work must scratch up a living somehow or other by means of his own efforts....Thus, except under peculiar conditions, a decline in effective demand which reduces the amount of employment offered in the general run of industries, will not lead to "unemployment" in the sense of complete idleness but will rather drive workers into a number of occupations—selling match-boxes in the Strand, cutting brushwood in the jungles, digging potatoes on allotments—which are still open to them...in all these occupations which the dismissed workers take up, their productivity is less than in the occupations that they have left.... The cause of this diversion, a decline in effective demand, is

exactly the same as the cause of unemployment in the ordinary sense, and it is natural to describe the adoption of inferior occupations by dismissed workers as disguised unemployment. If a revival of investment were to occur, dismissed workers would be called back from the hedge rows and the street kerbs into their normal occupations (207, pp. 61-2).

Mrs. Robinson's Explanation of Disguised Unemployment

Fig. 1.1 refers to labour employed in unionized industries. The labour supply unit SS is horizontal up to full employment N_F at the wage rate OW (fixed, we suppose, by collective bargaining). DD is the demand curve for labour when we have full employment. $D'D'$ is the demand curve during the depression. N_2N_F workers are unemployed. Fig. 1.2 shows self-employed labour in petty jobs like selling

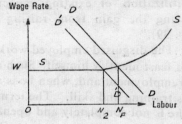

FIG. 1.1 LABOUR AS WAGE-EARNER IN UNIONIZED INDUSTRIES

apples, shining shoes, etc. DD is the demand curve for such services. The original level of earnings is OW for these jobs. With N_2N_F un-employment in unionized industries, SS in Fig. 1.2 shifts to the position $S'S'$ to absorb the unemployed. The level of earnings falls to OW_2. It will be observed that the marginal product (or wage rate) of N_2N_F workers was OW in their regular

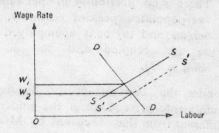

FIG. 1.2 SELF-EMPLOYED LABOUR

jobs, while they have been obliged to work in petty jobs with marginal product OW_2.

Mrs. Robinson's concept of disguised unemployment has only a limited relevance for underdeveloped countries:

(i) It is a cyclical phenomenon. With the revival of economic activity, workers return to more productive occupations and the problem will end. The loss of output is temporary and is due to the less than full utilization of existing skill and equipment. In an underdeveloped economy, however, the problem is not primarily that of a failure to utilize existing skills and the existing stock of capital. Although the technical skill that is available may not always be fully utilized, the main problem is one of increasing the supply of skill and rate of capital formation. As Bhabatosh Datta remarks : "It is not the negative problem of avoiding the waste of non-utilization of existing capacities, but the positive one of achieving the gain from raising the whole level of capacities (45, p. 39)."

(ii) The disguised employed worker, in Mrs. Robinson's sense, can at least identify himself. Such a person is aware of his state of underemployment and, when he is able, will resume work suited to his training and skill. The term "disguised" refers to the fact that he is not completely and openly idle. Some later economists have classified such a case as "visible underemployment."

In the family enterprise sector of underdeveloped economies in which family members participate in the production operations but not for wages, a part of the labour may be excessive. But as Nurkse points out:

> There is no possibility of personal identification here.... In an overpopulated peasant economy, we cannot point out to any person and say he is unemployed in disguise. The people may be all occupied and no one may consider himself idle (164, p. 33).

Under the circumstances, disguised unemployment in the family enterprise sector of the underdeveloped countries is quite different from that discussed by Mrs. Robinson.

Adopting Mrs. Robinson's notion of disguised unemployment to cover conditions in the underdeveloped countries Alfredo Navarrete, Jr. and Ifigenia M. de Navarrete (162) have come to the following conclusion :

> This type of cyclical underemployment also occurs in countries exporting primary products when external demand falls. Its magnitude is a direct function of the importance of foreign

trade in any particular country as well as of the relation between foreign trade and the country's domestic economy. Disguised unemployment will be greater, if the subsistence sector is more important which, generally, absorbs the excess labour and which serves as shock absorber for cyclical fluctuation of external demand. On the other hand, occurrence of visible unemployment will be more if the subsistence sector of the economy is less important (162, p. 342).

The possibility of some employment in the agricultural sector of underdeveloped countries caused by cyclical movements in the import demand of the industrial countries was also mentioned in *Measures for the Economic Development of Underdeveloped Countries* by the group of experts appointed by the United Nations (260, p. 5). They pointed out that the major effect of cyclical fluctuations on the agricultural sector in underdeveloped countries is the lowering of incomes rather than increased unemployment. Because of the very low price elasticity[1] of supply of most agricultural products, the volume of agricultural output, and thus also the volume of employment, are insensitive to price fluctuations.

One final remark is called for. It is argued that a decline in the level of spending would not result in unemployment if price and wage rates were perfectly flexible. If this proposition is accepted, then the downward rigidity of wages and prices—a structural element—would become a partial cause of the kind of unemployment which we associate with a deficiency of effective demand. Thus, the sharpness of our dichotomy between monetary and structural causes of unemployment is to some extent blurred. However, at the level of policy, the opportunities for significantly increasing wage and price flexibility may be extremely limited in the short period. In this context, therefore, little harm is done in contrasting the monetary and structural causes of disguised unemployment. We now consider these structural factors.

---

[1]PRICE ELASTICITIES OF ACREAGE UNDER SELECTED CROPS (ALL INDIA)

Rice	0.22	Wheat	0.16
Barley	0.16	Groundnut	0.22

National Council of Applied Economic Research, *Long Term Projections of Demand for and Supply of Selected Agricultural Commodities; 1960-61 to 1975-76*, p. 168

C. Disguised Unemployment Due to Imperfections in Particular Labour Markets

The term "disguised unemployment" has also been used in the literature to describe the situation of a worker whose marginal productivity in his present job is less than (*a*) other identical jobs somewhere else, or (*b*) other jobs for which he possesses suitable training and skill. Both these situations may arise from imperfections in the functioning of the competitive market mechanism, in particular, of labour markets. To understand the nature of disguised unemployment in this sense, it is helpful to visualize how perfectly competitive labour markets supposedly operate.

1 FULL EMPLOYMENT EQUILIBRIUM IN NEO-CLASSICAL ECONOMICS

For neo-classical economists, given:

(i) a perfect competition and price flexibility in both, factor and product markets,
(ii) profit maximization on the part of entrepreneurs, and
(iii) a sufficiency of aggregate demand, there will be a strong tendency towards full employment of all resources including labour.

Full employment is defined as the situation in which all labour inputs willing and able to work at the existing real wage level are employed. In this model, unemployment is not completely impossible, but is a disequilibrium position, and continues only long enough for the competitive forces to attain equilibrium.

The actual level of employment is determined by the demand and supply of labour. As for the demand function for labour, the entrepreneur's optimum input combination satisfies the condition that price of each input (money wage rate in the case of labour) equals the value of its marginal product. Each homogeneous category of labour input will be so allocated among different sectors of the economy that the value of its marginal product is equalized in all its uses, and all firms, in all sectors, pay a wage rate equal to the value of labour's marginal product. Any difference in marginal products or wage rates of homogeneous labour inputs in the different sectors will provide incentives to labour to move between sectors until the differential is eliminated, as shown in Fig. 1.3.

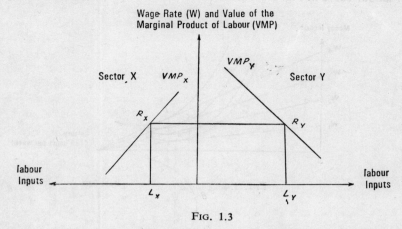

Fig. 1.3

In Fig. 1.3, we have two sectors X and Y with a marginal value product of labour function in each sector. The total labour force will be distributed in the two sectors so as to equalize the value of the marginal product of labour in the two sectors.

The supply of labour function of a single worker is derived from his offer curve for work and it indicates the number of hours he will work at various wage rates. With a view to maximizing his utility, an individual allocates his available time (the length of the period for which the utility function is defined) between work and leisure so that the ratio between the marginal utility of leisure and the marginal utility of income from work is equal to the wage rate. Where the supply function has a positive slope, this implies that the substitution effect of a wage rate increase outweighs the income effect, assuming that leisure is not an inferior good. Where the supply function is sloping backward, the income effect of a wage rate increase outweighs the substitution effect.

In Fig, 1.4, we have drawn an indifference map for two commodities—income and leisure. The number of hours of leisure per week are plotted on the horizontal axis and weekly income is plotted on the vertical axis. The straight lines radiating from the point 168 hours of leisure are exchange paths between leisure and income corresponding to different wage rates, W_1, W_2, etc. such that $W_4 > W_3 > W_2 > W_1 >$.

Projecting the tangency points, A,B,C,D gives us the individual's supply of labour curve in Fig. 1.5. This curve has the property of bending

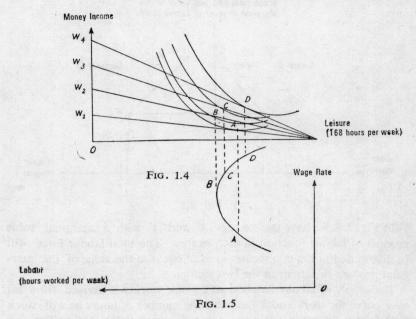

FIG. 1.4

FIG. 1.5

backward, indicating that, after a certain point, less labour is supplied at high wage rates than at low ones. The aggregate supply of labour of a homogeneous type is the sum of the individual supply schedules.

Given the demand and supply function for labour, the equilibrium wage rate and employment level combination is determined by invoking the equilibrium condition—labour demanded equals labour supplied. Any disequilibrium causing excess supply or excess demand is corrected by price flexibility in both, the factor and product markets.

The disguised unemployment of labour in specific labour markets may now be explained in terms of deviations from the assumptions of the model of the perfectly competitive mechanism.

2 IMMOBILITY OF LABOUR

Discussing the problem of disguised unemployment among farmers in the South-Eastern United States, C. E. Bishop States: "Labour is underemployed when the marginal real return received for labour in agriculture is less than the marginal real returns received for comparable labour in other uses (18, p. 1197)." Bishop admits that the "persistence of underemployment raises serious questions about the competitive character of the economy" (18, p. 1197). He mentions, that (*i*) non-availability of capital to finance the transfer of labour into other uses, and (*ii*) ignorance on the part of farmers of the opportunities for employment of labour in higher paying uses are two of the factors that discourage the movement of labour off the farms in sufficient numbers to equalize the real rates of return.

Ragnar Nurkse describes disguised unemployment in Latin American countries in similar terms:

> There are always some occupations that are relatively unproductive while others are relatively productive. A transfer of labour from the former to the latter would increase total output and so the people in the relatively unproductive occupations might in this sense be considered underemployed.

Irma Rittenhouse (206) also uses the term "disguised unemployment" in the same sense. The nature of disguised unemployment in this sense is illustrated in Fig. 1.6.

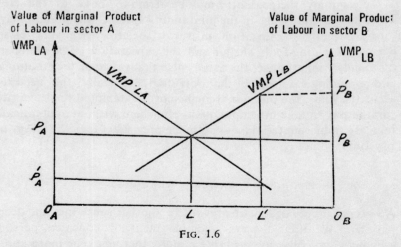

FIG. 1.6

In Fig. 1.6, we have total labour force $O_A O_B$ working in two sectors; in sector A, with marginal value product $V M P_{LA}$ and sector B, with marginal value product VMP_{LB}. Under the conditions of efficient utilization of labour, it would be allocated between the two sectors so that there was $O_A L$ in sector A and $O_B L$ in sector B with the marginal value product equal in the two sectors $(O_A P_A = O_B P_B)$. If there is O L' labour in sector B and $O_A L'$ in sector A, the marginal value products of labour will be different in the two sectors $(O_B P'_B, O_A P'_A)$. If LL' fails to move from sector A to sector B, this difference in the marginal products will continue and the labour LL' in sector A would be characterized as disguised unemployed. By taking appropriate steps to lessen the obstacles to mobility, the problem can be alleviated.

Disguised unemployment, in this sense, is not peculiar to underdeveloped economies. It can, as Bishop and Irma Rittenhouse have pointed out, occur in the developed economies as well. Nevertheless, the problem of labour immobility may be greater in the underdeveloped economies for several reasons. First, there is greater ignorance and illiteracy, along with a lack of effective media to transmit information regarding the availability of jobs in different areas in the country. Secondly, because of the great difference in the "pattern of living" in the urban and rural sectors of the economy, the peasantry may be afraid to move to the city. Thirdly, the family ties in the joint family system—the predominant form of family organization in rural societies—are very close. Besides providing food, shelter and the expectation of a share in the family's inheritance, the family also takes care of the emotional and psychological needs of the individual, especially the need for security. Thus, the individual might not be tempted to leave the joint family to take up employment elsewhere without a significant increase in his material income to compensate for the loss of psychic income.

3 ERRORS IN PLANNING VOCATIONAL TRAINING

An excess supply of labour prevails in another sense in some occupations. We often observe unemployment of educated persons seeking white-collar jobs. For example, there may be more applicants for clerical jobs than the vacant positions; there may be more PH. D's seeking positions as professors than there are openings. High school graduates may be compelled to accept positions as peons (a type of menial servants in offices). M. Bronfenbrenner (25) cites examples from the teaching profession in Japan. Some rural elementary schools include on their staff violently dissatisfied men and women with unusable graduate training in history, politics, economics, literature, philosophy, etc. These seemingly employed are anxious to shift to positions more appropriate to their education. Their skills and training are not being fully utilized and their marginal products in the present jobs are less than their potential marginal products. The terms "disguised unemployment" and "latent disguised unemployment" have been ascribed to these employment patterns. According to Bronfenbrenner, "disguised unemployment may also mean that many workers have skills, which they have little chance to use" (25).

A committee appointed by the President in 1961 to appraise the employment and unemployment statistics in the United States defined the concept as the "employment of persons at jobs that call for less than their highest current level of skill and at wages less than those to which their skills, if fully utilized, would normally entitle them" (261, p. 58). Louis J. Ducoff and Margaret J. Hagood use the term to describe "employment in jobs which permit only the partial utilization of their capabilities" (55, p.249). In Japan, this differential income and utilization of skill approach has been described by E. Ohata (168) as employment of a worker in a job not commensurate with his real ability, despite his desire to take a more skilled job. This point is also made by A. Yamanaka (273), I. Ohkawa (169), and W. Umemura (258). In Japan, information on the extent of latent disguised unemployment in respect of both, the self-employed and unpaid family workers, has been collected as part of a special survey of the labour force conducted on a monthly basis since October 1957 by the Bureau of Statistics (Office of the Prime Minister). Employed persons are asked whether they want to change jobs and if so, why ? Latent disguised unemployment is indicated if a person wishes to change jobs because his present job is inadequate owing to too low earnings, lack of skill utilization, etc.

Disguised unemployment, in this sense, is simply a case of excess labour supply arising out of disequilibrium in the demand and supply of particular types of labour. Under perfectly competitive conditions, the real wage rate in the higher paying occupations to which admission is sought would fall, causing more of such workers to be hired and also discouraging new entrants to these fields, thus eliminating the excess supply. For what reasons do real world markets fail to yield this solution? We need to answer two questions. First, what causes the excess supply of skill to come into existence? Second, why does this excess supply fail to induce a wage rate decline?

One answer to the first question may be that people enter schools and select fields of training, not always taking labour market conditions into consideration. Choice in the fields of education is determined, partly, by non-economic factors such as aptitudes, intellectual capacity and social status. Problems may arise from forecasting errors in planning vocational training. The wage rates for many such jobs are not flexible downwards. There may be some floor wage rates based on customary living standards. The excess supply of workers would thus fail to reduce the wage rates sufficiently to absorb them in these specific occupations. In these circumstances, the market mechanism would fail to solve the problem of "excess supply," and the "round pegs in the square holes" would continue to exist.

To view disguised unemployment in terms of underutilization of skills and income differentials has its limitations. First, there may not be a one-way relationship between income and skill. Is a person who was trained to be a teacher underemployed if he drives a truck, when his income as a truck driver is higher than it would be if he taught in a school? In many cases, the ordering of occupations in accordance with the social esteem attached to them correlated imperfectly with their ranking in terms of income. In such instances, a person in a job, carrying high remuneration but low social esteem, might like to shift to a job carrying higher social esteem but lower income. Will such a person be considered as unemployed in disguise? In underdeveloped countries like India, the social esteem of a job is governed by factors like caste or family group. Income, sometimes, plays a minor role. In India, some jobs considered menial from caste and social viewpoints and requiring little education or skill (raising hogs and poultry, street sweeping) pay a higher remuneration than jobs yielding higher social esteem and requiring comparatively high education (junior school teachers and junior clerks). These clerks and teachers could raise their incomes by shifting jobs but they would not think of doing so.   The difference in social prestige is more important to them than the difference in money income. Similarly, the raisers of hogs and poultry may wish to shift to some other jobs, even with a lower income.   Would we consider them as disguised unemployed?   Furthermore, in underdeveloped countries where the vast majority of peasants and agricultural workers are, at least, functionally illiterate, it is difficult to pinpoint their aptitudes and potential skills to determine whether or not they are utilizing their skills properly.   In view of these difficulties, the differential income or utilization of skill approach is of little value in analyzing and measuring the extent of disguised under-employment in the rural sectors of underdeveloped countries.

CHAPTER TWO

EXCESS AGGREGATE LABOUR SUPPLY AND DISGUISED UNEMPLOYMENT

THE DISGUISED unemployment, which is due to an excess aggregate labour supply relative to the aggregate supplies of cooperating inputs (land and capital), could exist even if there were no deficiency of aggregate demand and no imperfections in the adjustment processes in specific labour markets. Even a perfectly working market mechanism cannot provide a full employment solution to this set of initial conditions. The following paragraphs provide only a rough sketch of this argument, which will be developed in more detail later. At this stage we simply assume that each worker supplies a fixed number of man-hours of labour.

Case 1 (a)

Suppose, workers are hired by profit maximizing entrepreneurs and the productivity of each worker is, up to a point, an increasing function of his real wage. Postulate a minimum competitive real wage (W_C) below which a further reduction would lower the average productivity of each worker more than in proportion to the decline in real wage. The rational employer with perfect knowledge would not persistently reduce the real wage rate below this level even if unemployed workers offer to work for less. Define the subsistence wage rate (W_S) as the wage level below which the labour force would shrink through starvation. At this wage level, the labour force would remain stationary. A higher wage rate would increase the labour force. In Fig. 2.1, OL_1 is the total number of workers seeking work, and OW_C and OW_S are the minimum competitive and subsistence wage rates respectively. The marginal physical product curve contains within itself an allowance for the effect of a change in the real wage on workers' productivity. Profit maximizing entrepreneurs hire OL_2 workers at the minimum competitive wage rate and so L_2L_1 workers would be rendered unemployed. They are willing to work for a wage lower than the minimum competitive wage rate but since, at a lower wage rate, workers' productivity would be reduced more than in proportion to the decline in the real wage rate, the entrepreneur will not hire them.[1]

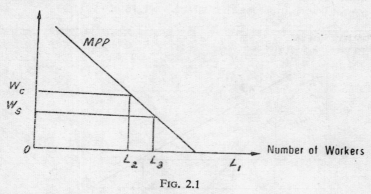

Fig. 2.1

These unemployed workers starve in the absence of any institutional arrangements for subsidizing them. The competitive market mechanism has, thus, not been able to solve the problem of unemployment except by waiting for the unemployed to vanish from the market.

Case 1 (b)

All the assumptions are the same as in Case 1 (a) except that labour productivity is now assumed to be independent of the real

[1]It could be urged that a firm could manage to pay a real wage rate lower than the "minimum competitive real wage rate" without loss of productivity. It then could hire only the healthy workers, pay them lower wages (lower than the competitive real wage rate), fire them when their marginal product fell below the real wage rate and hire new healthy workers again and so on. Our contention is that such a policy could work, but only until all the healthy workers have been thus used up by all the firms. Then some "minimum competitive real wage rate" would describe the long-run equilibrium. This wage might, alternatively be "social minimum" determined by " socially acceptable" stand-and of living and enforced as "minimum wage rate" by the Government.

wage rate.   The real wage rate in the short run will approach zero until L_3L_1 workers die, leaving, in the long run, equilibrium wage rate equal to OW_S and the labour force equal to OL_3.

Case 2 (a)

Suppose now, that all productive enterprises are organized on a family basis.   No workers are hired.   The joint family has an obligation to share its work and income with all its members. Assume again that the productivity of each worker increases up to a point with increase in his real wage rate:

Real Wage Rate and
Marginal and Average Product

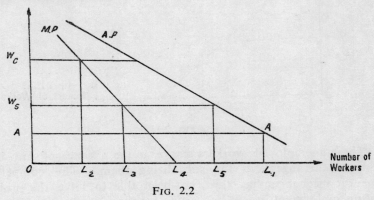

FIG. 2.2

In Fig. 2.2, OL_1 is the initial size of the labour force; MP and AP are the marginal and average product curves.   In the family enterprise, if all members share equally in the total income, the share of each would be OA.   Since OA is less than the subsistence wage rate OW_S, it cannot be maintained. The long-run equilibrium wage rate (defined as an equal share of the family's income) would then be OW_S received by OL_5 members, and L_5L_1 workers would starve.   In this case, L_2L_5 workers would be the disguised unemployed because, under perfectly competitive conditions, only OL_2 workers should be hired at OW_C wage rate. It may be noted that L_2L_5 disguised unemployed are of two categories.   The marginal product of L_4L_5 is zero, while it is positive but less than the minimum competitive wage rate OW_C in the case of L_2L_4 workers.

Case 2 (b)

All assumptions are the same as in Case 2 (a) except that the labour productivity is now assumed to be independent of the wage rate. The family would continue supporting OL_5 workers, each getting OW_S real wage rate. But the disguised unemployment would now be L_3L_5 because under perfectly competitive conditions, OL_3 workers would be hired at OW_S real wage rate. The marginal product of L_4L_5 is zero, while it is positive but less than the subsistence wage rate OW_S in the case of L_3L_4 workers.

Case 3 (a)

Assume that the work force is divided between two sectors; one organized on a family basis with no hired labour and the other on an impersonal basis in which workers are hired by profit maximizing entrepreneurs. The land and capital inputs are divided between the two sectors in such a way that the marginal return per rupee invested in each type of input is equalized in both sectors. Suppose also, that the productivity of each worker is an increasing function of the real wage rate:

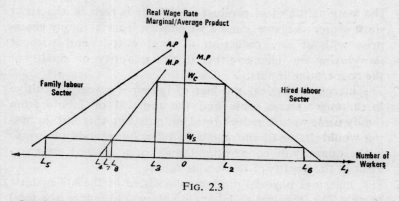

FIG. 2.3

On the right side of Fig. 2.3 is the hired labour sector with its MP curve. The total labour force is OL_1. At the minimum competitive wage rate OW_C, OL_2 workers would be hired and L_2L_1 workers would be unemployed. These unemployed workers would be supported by the family type enterprises in the left side of the diagram as OL_5 workers. Since OL_5 workers share the family's income, each would receive his average product which also coincidentally equals the subsistence wage rate OW_S. In this case, L_3L_5 workers are the disguised unemployed, consisting of L_3L_4 with positive marginal product and L_4L_5 with a zero marginal product.

Case 3 (b)

The assumptions are the same as in Case 3 (a) except that the productivity of workers is independent of the real wage rate. Continuing to use Fig. 2.3, the long-run equilibrium real wage rate in the "hired labour" sector would be OW_S at which OL_6 workers would be hired and L_6L_1 workers would be rendered unemployed and would shift to the family labour sector as OL_7. Now the number of disguised unemployed in the case is L_8L_7.

While these models clarify the fundamental characteristics of this type of disguised unemployment, the literature on the subject has evolved in a way which makes it difficult to fit a survey into exactly the same framework. Therefore, the study of the literature along the following assumptions is a necessity:

1 The marginal physical product of labour is zero in the strict static sense. Labour can be withdrawn from a family enterprise without any reduction in total output and without introducing any change either in the quantity or quality of the cooperating inputs.
2 The marginal physical product of labour is actually positive in the strict static sense and the removal of labour from family firms would reduce total output, but this fall in output would be small and could be offset by a modest increase in the quantity of cooperating inputs or a modest improvement in the quality of the labour input.
3 The marginal physical product is positive in the strict static sense. The removal of labour inputs would reduce the total output substantially and this fall cannot be offset by modest changes in the quantity or quality of cooperating inputs.

One possible criticism of the literature is that the theoretical distinction between the first and second of these three categories has not been made sufficiently explicit.

A. Disguised Unemployment where the Marginal Physical Product of Labour is Zero in the Strict Static Sense[2]

A zero marginal productivity of labour which is seasonal or for a short term is more easily explained than a zero marginal product which is permanent or chronic. Therefore, we shall first examine the time dimension of the zero marginal hypothesis.

1   THE TIME DIMENSION OF ZERO MARGINAL PRODUCTIVITY

In this section, we shall review the literature on the time-pattern of the phenomenon of disguised unemployment, i.e. the length of time for which the marginal product of the disguised unemployment is zero.

(a) Seasonal Disguised Unemployment: The seasonal rise and fall in farm activity is a general phenomenon in agriculture. Seasonality can be traced back to the time interval between the tasks of sowing and harvesting, to the rigid necessity of carrying out operations at the right time, and to the simultaneity of the harvest period for all cultivators in a particular region. The problem of seasonality is, thus, in the words of Howard, "the problem of inelasticities of the time-pattern of primary production (89*).*"

In agriculture, nothing is made or manufactured; everything has to grow and become. Thus, in agricultural operations, the period "off growth and maturity, followed by harvesting, together with an "off-season," account for a whole solar year. Both the rhythm and vagaries of the climatological and biological factors explain the seasonality. This seasonality—its peak and slack seasons—vitally affect the employment pattern in agriculture. In the off-season, practically, nothing can be done on the farm leading to enforced unemployment. On the other hand,

---

[2]As a part of the *ceteris paribus* assumption, we assume "currently applied" rather than "best known" technique cultivation. The labour inputs that could be spared by changing the "applied" technique would fall in Category 3 above. Disguised unemployment in this sense becomes just an alternative, perhaps, for the gap between the "known" and "applied" technique of cultivation. In the agricultural sector of an underdeveloped economy, this gap is, however, not very perceptible.

during the busy season, the farm workers may be overemployed—to finish work within a span of time determined by climatological and biological factors. This unemployment during the slack agricultural seasons has been referred to as "seasonal unemployment" by most writers on the subject, including Rosenstein-Rodan (210, 211), a U.N. group of experts (260), Navarrete (162), A. Chiang (29, 30), Nurkse (164), Cho (31), Mujumdar (156), Mukerji (157), Pepelasis (187). During the slack seasons, a part of the work force in agriculture becomes redundant and it could, perhaps, be utilized elsewhere without reducing the total output. Even those who are most sceptical regarding the general validity of the zero marginal productivity hypothesis, accept this seasonal notion of disguised unemployment. Viner (263) characterizes seasonal unemployment as a "realistic description" of agriculture. According to Duesenberry, "there is a large volume of disguised unemployment in agriculture due to the seasonal nature of agricultural operations," (56). Some further features of seasonal agricultural unemployment may be noted:

(1) The magnitude of seasonal unemployment varies with the type of crop-mix, condition of the soil, technique of cultivation, possibility of crop rotation, etc. Among agricultural operations, there are some which can be successfully performed only at certain times. Thus, in crop production, as pointed out by Mujumdar (156), there are, usually, two periods of "rush work"—sowing and harvesting—followed by the idleness of the "off-seasons" or "dead seasons."

There are other operations, however, such as hedging and general upkeep of farms and buildings, which can be done at any time during the year. There are still others which impose a routine throughout the year, such as milking, tending and caring for the livestock. Thus, the pattern of employment in "crop agriculture" differs from "livestock enterprise." "Rainfall agriculture" also differs from "irrigation agriculture." In "irrigation agriculture," there are many small "leisure-time jobs" that can be done with small intermittent inputs of labour, e.g. deepening drains, making or repairing ropes for water-raising operations, repairing and maintaining irrigation equipment, keeping the irrigation ditches free of weeds, etc. In the case of "rainfall agriculture," the timing and duration of agricultural operations depend on the rainfall cycle.

(2) It may be more appropriate to describe this seasonal unemployment as "visible" rather than "disguised" unemployment since during the "dead season," the farmer is aware of his state of inactivity and, according to Howard, "...is waiting to sow his ground, as spring comes around" (89). In his classification of unemployment in Asia, Hsieh Chiang (29, 30) treats this seasonal inactivity as "visible unemployment."

(3) The problem of seasonal unemployment is not peculiar to agriculture in the underdeveloped economies. It exists in most forms of productive enterprises. Using the adjective "disguised" to describe seasonal unemployment is, according to Viner, improper, as "...seasonal unemployment is a distinct phenomenon ...not obviously having any peculiar relationship to agriculture in underdeveloped countries" (263, p. 17). And, as Harvey Leibenstein states:

> ...the agricultural labor force may be said to suffer from disguised unemployment in the same sense that taxi-drivers may be said to suffer from disguised unemployment. During the daily peak periods, all taxis find riders and if there were additional taxis, they would find additional riders. But during other times of the day a great many of the taxis are idle. The hours of idleness may outweigh the hours during which they are delivering passengers. In this sense they may be said to be partially unemployed or to suffer from disguised unemployment (125, p. 60).

(4) Though seasonal unemployment is a world-wide phenomenon in agriculture, the problem is of much greater magnitude in the underdeveloped countries. First, because by far the largest proportion of their population is engaged in agriculture; and secondly, because, in these economies, there is a predominant dependence on rainfall agriculture. According to Nurkse, "seasonal underemployment is likely to be significant where an annual crop cycle (e.g. of cereal food crops) dominates farm activity and where this activity has not developed more advanced farms, such as dairy farming" (164, p. 35).

(5) P. K. Mukerji considers seasonal unemployment as "unavoidable and not serious[3] (157, p. 88), and Peter Bauer and Basil

---

[3] The seasonal unemployment is unavoidable in the sense that in the off agricultural season, there is no work to be done on the farm.

Yamey remark that seasonally unemployed workers should not be considered redundant, as:

> labor which seems to be performing no economic function during some months may in effect be supplying the service of availability; a machine is not necessarily redundant if it is not used in production all the time (8, p. 33).

For Philip Raup, the time of seasonal unemployment represents the "cost of production," as:

> The biological nature of agricultural production introduces a dimension that bears heavily on patterns of investment of family labor. Much of the "cost" of agricultural production is a time cost. Crops must ripen, animals must mature, and the principal part of the labor cost of these processes is the cost of waiting. Even in well-organized farm firms, there are substantial time periods in which the labor force must be on hand, but technically underemployed (203, p. 10).

(b) *Periodic Disguised Unemployment:* Whereas the term "seasonal" unemployment refers to a period of inactivity within a one-year crop cycle, "periodic" disguised unemployment relates to the possibility of removing a part of the labour force from the farms for several years, though not permanently, without reducing total output. The magnitude of such a labour surplus would depend on the extent to which maintenance activities could be deferred without an adverse effect on the output. The maintenance of irrigation ditches and wells, the periodic overhauling of agricultural implements, and the repair of cattle sheds are possible examples of such activities. Their temporary neglect might not show its adverse effect on total output for some years, during which period some labour could be removed for use elsewhere. William Barber (7) speaks of the possibility of withdrawing as much as 50 per cent of the able-bodied male workers for two to three years without affecting the total farm output through the division of farm labour in Africa. According to Barber, farm work is of two types: first, the routine work of sowing seeds, tending and reaping crops; and secondly, the other work—maintaining the productivity of the soil through shifting cultivation. In this method of land utilization, once a piece of land has lost its fertility through cultivation, it is replaced by new land, prepared for cultivation by clearing bush, burning it and allowing the ash to fertilize the soil, etc. This process of shifting cultivation takes two to three years. The routine work is performed by women, and the men undertake the other work. While the women workers are tied to the land all the year round, the male population can be withdrawn from the farms without reducing the total output for two to three years at a time.

(c) *Chronic Disguised Unemployment:* The term "chronic disguised unemployment" (also used in the literature interchangeably with terms such as "chronic surplus labour," and "structural hidden unemployment"), according to the Navarretes, indicates:

> A situation in which the withdrawal of a certain quantity of the factor labor to other uses will not appreciably diminish the total output of the sector from which it is withdrawn. This is as much to say that the marginal productivity of those units of the factor labor in their original employment is zero or very close to zero (162, p. 341).

The time period for removal of workers without reducing the total output is laid down as at least one complete year (to distinguish it from the seasonal phenomenon) by Rosenstein-Rodan (210, 211) and Adam A. Pepelasis and Pan A. Yotopoulos (187). According to Hsieh Ching (29, 30), the test of chronic disguised unemployment lies in the excessive supply of labour time even at the peak of agricultural activity. Doreen Warriner (265) claimed to have found chronic disguised unemployment in her studies in Europe in 1936. In 1943, a committee on reconstruction set up under the auspices of the Royal Institute of International Affairs (217) undertook the task of measuring the surplus population in agriculture in eastern and south-eastern Europe. In this report, the committee estimated percentages of surplus farm population in Poland, Czechoslovakia, Rumania, Hungary and Greece, over and above the seasonal unemployment. Rosenstein-Rodan (210) estimated in 1943, the disguised unemployment in the eastern and southern Europe at 100 to 110 million—25 per cent of the total agrarian population. Mandelbaum built the case for industrialization of densely populated countries upon the existence of mass disguised unemployment. The surplus manpower, according to Mandelbaum, is an asset for these countries, since "...if these surplus workers were withdrawn from agriculture and absorbed into other occupations, farm output would not suffer, while new output would be a net addition to the community's income" (135, p. 2). In suggesting measures for economic development of under-developed economies, a group of experts[4] appointed by the United Nations in May 1951, recommended remedies for chronic disguised unemployment, which they defined as:

> Persons who are so numerous, relatively to the resources with which they work, that if a number were withdrawn for work in other sectors of the economy, the total output of the sector from which they were withdrawn would not be diminished even though no significant reorganization and no significant substitution of capital occurred in this sector (260, p. 7).

The concept of disguised unemployment in the sense of zero marginal productivity of labour, according to Nurkse, applies only to densely populated countries. Referring to thinly populated countries in Latin America, Nurkse writes:

> There is little or no evidence to show that South America has much disguised unemployment in the sense that, without any change in methods, large masses of manpower could be drawn away from food production without affecting the volume of output there (164, p. 50).

W. Arthur Lewis, in 1954, presenting his famous model of capital formation and development in which the capitalist sector grows by drawing on cheap rural labour, assumes an unlimited supply of labour in densely populated countries like Egypt, India, or Jamaica, "where population is so large relatively to capital and natural resources that there are large sectors of the economy where the

---

[4]The group was composed of:

  (1) Professor Alberto Baltra Cortez, National University of Chile,
  (2) Professor D. R. Gadgil, Director Gokhale Institute of Politics and Economics, Poona, India,
  (3) Mr. George Hakim, Counselor, Legation of Lebanon, Washington D. C.,
  (4) Professor W. Arthur Lewis, University of Manchester, England, and
  (5) Professor Theodore W. Schultz, University of Chicago.

marginal productivity of labour is negligible, zero, or even negative" (130, p. 402). R. S. Eckaus made reference to the large agrarian population in much of Asia and the Middle East "with marginal productivity of the working force so low that it is commonly believed that withdrawal of a sizeable fraction would not significantly affect output" (57, p. 348). John W. Mellor and Robert K. Stevens (140), N. Georgeseu-Roegen (67), William Barber (7), V. K. R. V. Rao (200), C. N. Vakil and Brahmanand (262), A. K. Sen (225, 226), Rosenstein-Rodan (210, 211), Shigeto Tsuru (262), and Alan H. Gleason (71), all subscribe to the view of chronic disguised unemployment with zero marginal productivity of labour in the rural sector of underdeveloped countries.

2 THEORETICAL BASIS FOR THE ZERO MARGINAL PRODUCT HYPOTHESIS

In this section we shall discuss the logic of the zero marginal product hypothesis in the strict static sense.

The zero marginal product of agricultural workers during the "slack" or "off season" is explained by both the rhythm and vagaries of climatological and biological factors affecting agriculture. In the "dead season," little can be done on the farms, and part of the labour force can thus be withdrawn during this season without reducing the total output.

In this case of periodic disguised unemployment, a part of the work force may be withdrawn for some period, while maintaining the total output, provided that maintenance activities can be deferred without adverse effect on the output.

As regards the explanation for the existence of zero marginal product on a chronic basis, the much-quoted "limited opportunities for technical substitution of factors and inappropriate factor endowments," hypotheses of R. S. Eckaus provide one logical foundation. According to Eckaus: "There have been frequent comments which describe certain features of underdeveloped and overpopulated areas as essentially the result of limited variability in the coefficients of production" (57, p. 355). The case of "limited opportunities for technical substitution of factors" is illustrated in Fig. 2.4.

In Fig. 2.4, the range of substitution of labour and capital in the product isoquants is between the ridge lines ON and OM.

Beyond these ridge lines, the marginal rate of technical substitution between the inputs becomes zero. Suppose we have a fixed

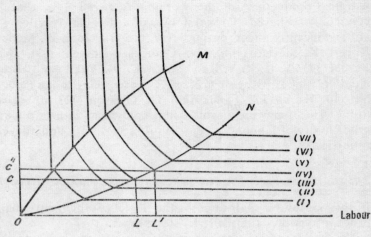

Fig. 2.4

amount of capital input OC and labour OL'. With OC capital we can productively employ only OL labour input by extending the output level to isoquant No. 111. For full employment of total labour OL', an increase in the capital to C" is essential. If the increased supply of capital is not forthcoming and the total labour force OL' is working on the farms, LL' labour inputs would be redundant with zero marginal product.

The idea of limited opportunities for technical substitution in agriculture over a particular range is not new. It is hinted at in the writings of the earlier economists. David Ricardo hinted at the notion of the surplus population in his statement, "with population pressing against the means of subsistence, the only remedies are either a reduction of people or more rapid accumulation of capital" (204, p. 76). The Marxian concept of an "industrial reserve army," according to Masao Fukoka, implies an excess of available labour over the level of employment determined by the amount of capital and the fixed capital coefficient per unit of labour employed (65, p. 25). Doreen Warriner seems to imply "fixed technical coefficients" in his statement on peasant farming in Europe.

...the limits of labor intensification are quickly reached when no addition to capital can be made...thus to say that a region is overpopulated means simply that the working population is excessive with reference to a certain technique of cultivation (265, pp. 65-6).

(*a*) *Criticisms of the Assumption of Fixed Technical Coefficients in Agriculture:* The initial attack came from Jacob Viner, who challenged the assumption of fixed technical coefficients in general and in agriculture in particular:

> I am not aware that any one has ever given a convincing illustration of a technical coefficient which is "fixed" in a valid economic sense.... As far as agriculture is concerned, I find it impossible to conceive of a farm of any kind on which, other factors of production being held constant in quantity and even in form as well, it would not be possible by known methods, to obtain some addition to the crop by using additional labor in more careful selection and planting of seeds, more intensive weeding, cultivation, thinning and mulching, more painstaking harvesting, gleaning, and cleaning of the crop. Even supposing that there was such a farm on which every product had technically and economically fixed ingredients, labour would still have positive marginal productivity, unless there were not only fixed technical coefficients of production for all economically relevant potential products of the farm, but the proportions between the technical coefficients were uniform for all of these products. For, if these proportions are different as between different products, then it will always be possible by appropriate changes in the product mix, in the direction of more production of those products whose labor technical coefficients are relatively high, to absorb productively any increment labor (268, p. 18).

Hence, "there is little or nothing in all the phenomena designated as disguised unemployment" (263. p. 18). Citing Brazilian plantations with "peasant and squatter agriculture" where the owners of the plantations felt a "shortage of hands," Viner remarks: "I don't see how this can be reconciled with the prevalence of zero marginal productivity of labor, whether on the plantations or for self-employed agricultural labor (263 p. 19)."

Whether the conditions of fixed technical coefficients of production exist on the farms in a particular country or not is a matter of empirical research rather than a logical issue and, unfortunately, Viner does not criticize specifically the many empirical studies purporting to show the existence of disguised unemployment. The Brazilian case cited by Viner does not give details about the type of labour for which the shortage was felt.

Denial of the importance of chronic disguised unemployment based on the assumption of fixed technical coefficients of production has also been voiced by eminent economists like Gottfried Haberler (76) and Theodore W. Schultz (221-4). According to Haberler, it is preposterous to assume that the technical coefficients are fixed (or that the production function isoquants are of rectangular or at least of angular shape) in the agriculture of a primitive economy as a chronic situation (76, p. 232). It may be pointed out that Haberler does not criticize empirical studies supporting opposite conclusions.

Theodore W. Schultz (221-4) has also been a strong critic of disguised unemployment with zero marginal productivity of surplus farm labour, both on the ground of its logic and its relevance to study the theory of economic development. He characterizes disguised unemployment as "an illusion,"..."a piece of the aftermath of the mass unemployment of the late thirties." He challenges fixed technical coefficients in agriculture or the "technological restraint hypotheses" of Eckaus as an explanation of zero marginal productivity of labour, remarking:

I know of no evidence for any poor country anywhere that would even suggest that a transfer of some small fraction, say, 5 per cent, of the existing labor force out of agriculture with other things equal, could be made without reducing production (221, p. 426).

According to Schultz:

...given the wide range for substitution among factors so characteristic of agriculture, it is all but impossible to construct even a theoretical model which would permit the possibility of a zero marginal product for an appreciable part of the labor supply (222, p. 375).

Schultz concludes that the overpopulation theory of underemployment as "theory...fails in that the expected consequences are not those one observes," (223, p. 15). In support of his contention, Schultz cites the following cases:

(*i*) In Peru a modest road was built down the eastern slopes of the Andes to Tingo Maria, using some labour from farms along the way, mostly within walking distance; agricultural production in the area dropped promptly because of the withdrawal of this labour from agriculture.

(*ii*) In Belo Horizonte, Brazil, an upsurge in construction in the city drew workers to it from the nearby countryside, and this reduced agricultural production.

In regard to these examples, we need more detailed empirical evidence before we conclude that it was really the withdrawal of labour that caused the fall in production. During which agricultural season was labour withdrawn? How much labour was withdrawn? Did other conditions such as climate, capital investment, etc. remain constant? These points need to be investigated further. It should also be noted that Viner and Schultz have cited examples from Latin America, where disguised unemployment (with zero marginal productivity) is commonly believed to be small. Even Nurkse (164, p. 50) specifically doubted the existence of disguised unemployment in the above sense in south American countries. Nicholas Georgeseu-Roegen, also writing about the disguised unemployment problem in Latin America resulting from overpopulation and accompanied by zero marginal productivity remarks:

The situation of most Latin American countries is not identical with that of the East European or Asiatic countries, although they all have this in common; they are underdeveloped. While overpopulation is always accompanied by underemployment, it is neither a necessary nor the only cause of it (67, p. 14).

It is not clear whether Viner, Haberler and Schultz are disputing the conceptual possibility or the empirical existence of a zero marginal product of labour in agriculture. Certainly, the empirical issue cannot be decided on the basis of the casual evidence which they offer. On the purely theoretical level, a sharper evaluation of their position is possible by repeating a small part of the excerpts from Schultz quoted above: "It is all but impossible to construct even a theoretical model which would permit the possibility of zero marginal product for an appreciable part of the labor supply (222, p. 373)."

If the intent of this statement was not descriptive but purely theoretical, then it seems invalid. Imagine a farm of fixed acreage and with fixed quantities of other non-labour inputs. Adding larger and larger amounts of labour, there must be some finite quantity at which total product cannot be further increased. The millionth worker will not increase the output from one acre of land. Graphically, this "self-evident" position can be illustrated as shown in Fig. 2.5.

All non-labour inputs

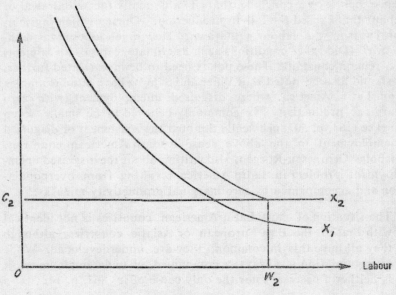

FIG. 2·5

If non-labour inputs are limited to C_2, there will be come finite quantity of labour OW_2 such that the relevant isoquant becomes horizontal at the points C_2W_2. Incidentally, this is not a fixed coefficient type production function (which is legitimately criticized by Viner, Haberler and Schultz as inappropriate in an agricultural context) but a variable proportions function. There is nothing in the classical production theory which denies that a sufficiently large increase in one input can reduce its marginal product to zero.

Probably, however, Viner, Haberler and Schultz were contesting the observability and not the conceivability of a zero marginal product. It may be appropriate, therefore, to indicate at this point some of the empirical studies on both sides of the issue, though the detailed evaluation of some of these studies is postponed to Chapter IV. The following studies indicate positive marginal productivity of farm workers:[5]

(*i*) John W. Mellor and T. V. Moorti, on the basis of their farm business analysis of 30 farms in Midhekur, a village in Agra District in Uttar Pradesh (India), during the year 1959, come to the conclusion that a "substantial increase in yields is possible through greater and more effective application of labour" (141, p. 26).

(*ii*) David W. Hopper's farm inquiries in the Uttar Pradesh (India) show that the marginal productivity of labour is positive (142, p. 11).

The following studies and observations indicating zero marginal productivity of surplus agricultural labour may be cited:

(*i*) John W. Mellor and Robert D. Stevens (140) studying the statistical relationship of the yield of rice to labour input in 104 rice farms in Beng Chan, a village in Thailand, in 1948, estimated an approximately zero marginal productivity of labour.

(*ii*) K. S. Gill (70), analyzing the problem of disguised unemployment in the underdeveloped countries found complementarity of resources in agricultural production causing disguised unemployment.

(*iii*) K. S. Suryanarayan (244) in his production function studies of agriculture in Andhra Pradesh (India) in 1958, computed the marginal product of labour as 0.93 and 0.22 per month

---

[5]From the numerous studies on the marginal product of labour as a test of disguised unemployment, we have quoted a few to illustrate the cases of positive and zero marginal products of labour.

(approximately zero) on irrigated and dry farms respectively.

(*iv*) In his production function studies of Japanese agriculture, Keizo Tsuchiya (254) found zero marginal productivity of labour for certain agricultural products, especially rice.

(*v*) S. Maruta (157), after a careful analysis of the accounts of 30 farms, which did not use mechanical power, in one of the poorest provinces of Japan, with an average labour input of 2700 man-hours per hectare, found a marginal return per man-hour of labour of only 0.064 kg. milled rice (0.075 kg. wheat equivalent)—a marginal productivity close to zero.

(*vi*) Colin Clark (32, p. 67) mentions cotton-growing in Soviet Uzbekistan as having labour inputs varying from 238 to 348 man-days per hectare per year, with no significant difference in yield, i.e. a zero marginal productivity on some farms. Clark does not indicate whether the land was of uniform quality in all these farms. There is also no mention of the capital equipment on the farms.

(*vii*) Earl O. Heady (82, p. 519) explains the decline of farm labour in the United States' major grain-producing regions with reference to a supplementary relationship between land and labour (with given capital) over a certain range of the production isoquant, implying that the marginal rate of substitution between two inputs is zero.

(*viii*) Leonard E. Hubbard in his studies of Soviet agriculture concluded:

The overpopulation of the agricultural district was vividly illustrated during the war. In 1916, when about 40 per cent of the able-bodied male peasants were in the army and some 2.6 million horses had been taken from agriculture for military purposes, farming operations were perfectly efficiently carried on by those who remained (90, p. 50).

Hubbard has not indicated whether any change in the farm organization was introduced in these farms.

(*ix*) Rosenstein-Rodan (211) cites an empirical confirmation of the phenomenon of disguised unemployment in the history of agricultural output in Poland during the Second World War. The agricultural output of German-occupied Poland during the Second World War did not fall when 20 per cent of the agricultural population was moved to the refugee and POW camps for forced labour. He does not mention whether the Germans introduced any change in farm organization in that area.

(x) A. R. Prest studied the impact of the Second World War on the economic conditions of primary-producing countries. Analyzing conditions in India, Prest gives information about the manpower that was directed to the war effort. He estimates the increase in public and private employment at 5 persons per million (190, pp. 29-30), of which the Indian Armed Services (Army, Navy and Air Force) alone account for 2.37 million. It can be assumed that rural areas contributed most of the increase to the armed services. Against this withdrawal of manpower from rural areas, Prest finds that the area of cultivated land, output per acre, and the extent of cropping over the period, 1939-45 more or less, remained constant (190, p. 38).

The above conclusions represent a sample of numerous studies on factor proportion relations, including the nature of technical coefficients of production in agriculture. The mere mention of these studies by no means implies acceptance of the accuracy of all their conclusions. After examining both the arguments and the results of empirical studies, the present writer feels that the question of, whether or not, the situation of fixed technical coefficients of production exists on farms at any particular place (and accordingly, whether the marginal product of labour there must fall to zero as the labour force rises) is a matter for empirical research. As Eckaus remarks, the hypothesis of limited substitutability of factors is one which "can be tested empirically and which deserves to be given factual content. Empirical testing requires measurement of the proportions in which productive factors can be and are actually used" (57, p. 375). In our opinion, the theoretical possibility of one variable input (e.g. labour) becoming absolutely redundant (with zero marginal product) at a certain stage with constant quantities of cooperating inputs (land and capital) to a fixed land input seems self-evident. But whether such a situation actually exists or not, cannot be decided by theoretical arguments.

It may also be pointed out that the challenge of fixed technical coefficient by Viner, Haberler and Schultz, is based on the denial of the possibility of strictly zero marginal product of the disguised unemployed worker. Schultz, however, accepts that "the productivity of labour is in general very low...because of the factors at the disposal of the community" (224, p. 56). It is interesting to note that some of the proponents of the "fixed technical coefficient" restraint do not insist on strict "zero marginal product." According to Eckaus, the marginal productivity of agrarian populations in the underdeveloped areas of the world, "is so low that it is commonly believed that the withdrawal of a sizeable fraction would not significantly affect output" (57, p. 349). Other economists use the expressions "zero or negligible," and "zero or approximately zero." According to Schultz, the main source of confusion lies in not recognizing the difference between "strict zero" and "approximately zero" or "negligible" marginal product. In his words:

> ...the productivity of labor is in general very low (and) misleads the casual observer who is accustomed to measuring margins in dollars. For him the difference between the penny-like margin and zero is at best difficult to discern. He is not likely to see margins that are worth only a penny, though these margins are real and relevant in such an economy (224, p. 56).

The issue, however, is not one that can be decided on the basis of *a priori* reasoning. Whether the marginal product of labour has or has not fallen in a particular agricultural community to the level which the farmers themselves deem to be "penny-like," is a question that can only be answered, if at all, by empirical investigation.

(b) *Logical Difficulties Raised by the Zero Marginal Product Hypothesis*: The purpose of this section is to explore some of the purely theoretical difficulties implicit in the zero marginal product hypothesis. It is convenient to start with the assumption that labour is so abundant, relative to other inputs that the last man-hour of available labour would add nothing to farm output. Then, to make this assumption tenable merely as a logical model, its proponents must be able to answer the following questions.

(i) Why should a self-employed farmer work for the marginal hour which adds nothing to the total output? Why is family labour worked to the point where no marginal return is forthcoming?

(ii) Why should the employer of hired labour pay positive wages to the labourer [whose product is zero or negligible? Why is the real wage higher than the marginal product? If a significant number of workers have a zero marginal product, should not the real wage be bid down to that marginal product of labour?

(c) *Zero Marginal Productivity of Labour on the Family Farm*: Institutions like the structure and social obligations of a joint family system (or extended family system) can be visualized as disguising the unemployment of family farm workers with zero marginal product.

According to the U. N. group of experts (260), the phenomenon is limited to self-employed farmers of "family-employment" as the group calls it. Taking an example from the Indian family system, Nurkse explains:

An essential element of the system is the Indian practice of sharing food, shelter and other necessities among distant as well as close relatives living together in peasant households. The marginal members of the farm labour force, if their own contribution to output falls short of their intake as customers, are subsidized by the rest of the community. In such circumstances, the marginal productivity of labor may easily be zero (166, p. 191).

He suggested that this type of unemployment is 'disguised' as opposed to 'open', in an industrial economy in the sense that:

...a number of people are working on farms or small peasant plots, contributing virtually nothing to output....There is no possibility of personal identification here as there is in open industrial unemployment....In an overpopulated peasant economy, we cannot point to any person and say he is unemployed in disguise. The people may all be occupied and no one may consider himself idle (164, p. 33).

This leads to a situation in which many workers merely "appear to be working." Thus, a special artificial kind of full employment prevails.

Majumdar explains the institutional matrix of the joint family system leading to disguised unemployment:

> In many of the underdeveloped economies, agriculture is characterized by the family-operated farms. Family rather than the individual is, thus, the employment unit in agriculture of those countries....Almost every member of the family is associated in varying degrees with the production on the farm; and the farm work by its very nature is such that the entire system and technique of production adopt themselves to the abundance of farm workers....In a rural society, family also acts as a pool into which all the earnings of members flow, and from which each individual gets a share according to his contribution of family occupation....In spite of the disguised unemployment, telling heavily upon the level of incomes, members of the family continue to till the land (156, pp. 48-9).

This view is also supported by Lewis (129, 130), Charles (36), Walter Neale (163), M. L. Gupta (74), L. N. Thaker (249), P. K. Mukerji (157), A. K. Sen (225, 226), V. K. R. V. Rao (200), Vakil and Brahmanand (262).

This social obligation of a joint family to maintain its members, irrespective of their contribution to the family's total earnings, possibly permitting a zero marginal product of labour, has been denied by Yong Sam Cho: "But the possibility of an unconditional automatic apportioning of the family's total output cannot seriously be entertained" (31, p. 43). Berdj Kenadjian also expresses doubt while remarking, "everyone getting an equal share whether they work or not seems hard to believe" (115, p. 55). Perhaps, in different cultures, the member's obligations and rights with respect to the joint or extended family's work and earnings differ. But in the Indian joint family system, the present writer agrees to G. B. Jather and S. G. Beri's statement:

> ...generally we may say that the joint family secures the advantage of simple division of labour to some extent, by giving each member such work as is suited to him....The infirm, in spite of their disability, are made to fit into the household economy,

being assigned work suited to their strength and capacity (III, p. 8).

As to the member's right to share the family's earnings, Jather and Beri's assertion: "the earnings of every member are thrown into the common stock, from which they are drawn as required by the head of the family to meet the needs of the family. Everyone earns according to capacity and receives according to need (111, p. 88)" describes the condition obtaining in Indian rural society.

The fact that the family rather than the individual is the employment unit in agriculture in many countries explains why unemployment can take a disguised rather than an overt form. The mechanism of calculating the marginal product in the sequential hiring of employees to match it with the wage rate, does not operate in the case of family members who work collectively on the family farm. In this connection, the marginal product of the collective effort could be zero in the sense that even if an able-bodied member of the family added nothing to the family output, he would nevertheless share both the work and the joint income. This, of course, is precisely the disguise which the unemployment takes. The emergence of the phenomenon in this sense has been explained in Cases 2 (a), 2 (b), 3 (a) and 3 (b) in the beginning of this chapter.

This still leaves unanswered, however, the original and basic question : Why should the members of a family work to the point where the marginal product of the last hour of labour becomes zero ? Yong Sam Cho phrases the difficulty thus:

If one takes the view that overpopulation results in the use of unnecessary labor, one implies wholesale irrationality on the part of the people of underdeveloped agricultural communities. Are these people really so irrational as habitually to apply labor unnecessarily (31, p. 14) ?

This question, according to A. K. Sen

...arises because of not distinguishing between labour and labourer. It is not that too much labour is being spent in the production process, but that too many labourers are spending it. Disguised unemployment, thus, normally takes the form of smaller number of working hours per head per year; for example, each of three brothers shepherding the sheep every third day. It is thus, the marginal productivity of the labourer, so to say, is nil over a wide range and the productivity of labour may be just equal to zero at the margin. It may also take the form of lower intensity of work with people "taking it easy," e.g. the peasant having time to watch the birds while working. If a number of labourers went away, the others would be able to produce the same output working longer and harder. There is no contradiction between disguised unemployment and rational behaviour (226, p. 15).

Sen's argument can be illustrated in Fig. 2.6.

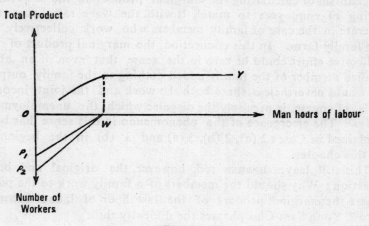

FIG. 2.6

The marginal physical product of labour becomes zero at OW man-hours of labour and labour is not applied beyond this point. The working population is OP_2, each putting in OW/OP_2 hours of work. OW/OP_1 represents the "normal" number of working hours per labourer. So the job can be done by OP_1 labourers working "normal hours." Thus, P_1P_2 of the labour force represents the volume of disguised unemployment.

Sen's explanation goes far towards rationalizing the zero marginal product model, but still leaves the following questions unexplained:

(*i*) Why would the working member of a family farm put in a total number of man-hours of work equal to OW, when the last small time interval worked by each worker yields a marginal product approaching zero? Would not the marginal utility of leisure cause the family to work a number of man-hours smaller than OW?

(*ii*) The quantity, the "normal" number of man-hours per worker, appears to be an exogenous quantity and is not obviously consistent with the theoretical principle that a worker prefers to work the number of hours such that the utility added by the income from the last hour of work just balances the marginal utility yielded by the last hour of leisure. This labour supply quantity depends, at the least, on some consensus of preferences among the family workers and is not some arbitrary "normal quantity."

Can these difficulties be resolved? It is possible to construct a logically consistent model in which man-hours or labour will be supplied to the point where the marginal physical product of labour actually drops to zero. This model depends on the plausible notion that *initial* hours of work afford a *positive* marginal utility, quite apart from the utility yielded by the income from that work.

In discussing the work-leisure preferences of workers, economists have tended to stress only the marginal disutility of work. In this sense, they have over-emphasized the economic aspect of work motivation to the neglect of non-economic factors that induce people to work. Friedman (64) mentions "income, regulating of life activity, identification, association and meaningful life experience, as the five functions of work." Nancy Morse and R. S. Weiss, on the basis of a survey of work attitudes of a random sample of employed men in the United States, list "enjoyment from work, association with people, keeping occupied, justification of one's existence, feeling of self-respect, and keeping healthy and active...besides income, as the positive reasons for working." They list "feeling lost, going crazy, feeling useless and bored, habit inertia, keeping out of trouble," as the results of not working (146, p. 31). Besides their personal feelings of loneliness, uselessness, and isolation, men without work are subject to social disapproval as "idlers, vagabonds, and dangerous.

If these views are translated into the formal terms of economic theory, we obtain a marginal utility of leisure function of the type shown in Fig. 2.7. The last hour of leisure in a maximum total of 24 hours per day yields a negative marginal utility which is the reflection of the positive marginal utility afforded by the initial hours of work exclusive of the utility from the product of that work.

Imagine, for example, a farm from which a large family is deriving its subsistence. The number of homogeneous family workers is large relative to the quantity of land and capital. Assume that each individual worker finds that after four hours of labour (assuming that the other family workers also are working four hours each), his marginal product falls to zero. Four hours of work leave twenty hours of leisure. At the level of twenty hours of leisure, the marginal utility of leisure falls to zero. We have a situation where each individual is working for four hours (with zero marginal product) and equating the marginal utility of leisure and work, thus, exhibiting rational economic behaviour in choosing between leisure and income. This case is illustrated in the diagram below.

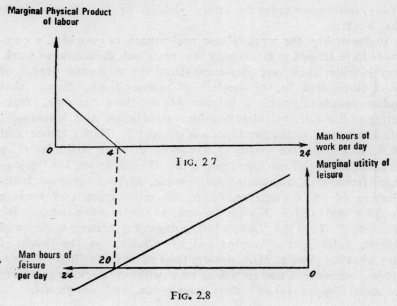

FIG. 2.8

In Fig. 2.7, we show man-hours of work per day on horizontal axis and marginal physical product on the vertical axis. In Fig. 2.8, the marginal utility of leisure is shown. The marginal product becomes zero after four hours of work and the marginal utility of leisure for the remaining twenty hours of leisure also falls to zero, thus equating the zero marginal utility of the additional product yielded by the last unit of time worked with the zero marginal utility of the last small unit of leisure time.

One shortcoming of the preceding model is that it assumes a coincidence of the points in time at which the marginal product of labour and the marginal utility of leisure become zero. A less restrictive case would be where the marginal product of labour becomes zero at a point in time when the marginal utility of leisure is still negative. This is illustrated in Figs. 2.9 and 2.10.

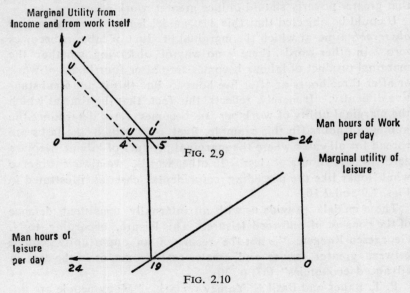

In Fig. 2.9 the broken line UU represents the marginal utility yielded by the output of successive man-hours of work. This is assumed to become zero after four hours of work. Adding to this marginal utility, the marginal utility (initially positive) associated with work *per se* yields the solid line U'U'. This combined marginal utility is assumed to become zero after five hours of work. These assumptions yield a preferred equilibrium of five hours of work and nineteen hours of leisure per day. At first sight, this solution does not make sense. How can one work a fifth hour if there is no product at all to show for it? There is however, a simple intuitive explanation. The time actually taken by a given person to perform a specific task tends, at least, for many workers, to vary widely depending on the strength of the incentives to finish sooner or later. In the above example, the incentives operate to induce the worker to spread over five hours the completion of tasks which he could comfortably (and without any decline in the quality of performance) have finished in four hours. This phenomenon may explain partially, at least, why in poor countries work habits seem more leisurely than in advanced countries. This seems paradoxical since one is tempted to deduce that greater poverty should induce greater work effort.

It could be objected that this last model leaves one without an *observable* time at which the marginal product of labour becomes zero. In other words, there is no way of observing whether the marginal product of labour becomes zero after four hours of work or after three hours or after five hours. But this is not a substantive difficulty. It merely reflects the fact that the time at which the marginal utility of work *per se* becomes zero determines the number of hours (in this example, five) over which the tasks are spread for all cases where the marginal product of labour becomes zero in five hours or less. In other words, we always observe what looks like the preceding coincidental case as illustrated in Figs. 2.9 and 2.10.

These models provide us with an internally consistent defence of the concept of enforced leisure. This leisure, according to N. Georgeseu-Roegen: "is not the result of an opportunity choice between greater leisure and greater real income, as in the case in advanced economies" (67, p. 30).

P. T. Bauer and Basil S. Yamey remark: "Many people are unemployed or underemployed not because they prefer idleness to work but because there is an insufficiency of cooperative factors of production to set them to work" (8, p. 74).

Explaining the nature of leisure in an underdeveloped economy Georgeseu-Roegen writes:

In strictly overpopulated countries, people have no choice: in those countries leisure is imposed upon them by geo-historical conditions....In a strictly overpopulated economy, leisure is not, properly speaking, an economic good, for it has no use but as leisure. Its value then can be zero (67, p. 30).

He characterized this leisure as "unwanted leisure" since the worker who is not obtaining any real income from further effort, resigns himself to the state of idleness. Elaborating on this unwanted leisure, Philip Raup (202) suggests the term "enforced leisure" resulting from "too few accessible productive resources with which to work."

(d) *Zero Marginal Productivity of Hired Farm Labour.* Under the assumptions of perfectly competitive labour market, the existence of unemployed workers with zero marginal product would theoretically reduce the real wage rate to the zero level. But, as explained in Cases 1 (a), (b) and 2 (a), (b) in the beginning of this chapter, the long-run equilibrium wage rates would tend to be either at subsistence level (assuming that productivity is unrelated to wage level) or equal to the competitive minimum wage rate (assuming that productivity is an increasing function of wage level), and an entrepreneur would hire labour to the point where its marginal product is equal to the wage rate. In such a situation, it is difficult to visualize the employment of hired farm labour whose marginal product is zero. This is, perhaps, why the United Nations group of experts excluded "wage labour" from "disguised unemployment" (with zero marginal product), remarking that "employers will not employ a laborer for wage labor unless his labor increases the total product" (260, p. 7). The phenomenon, according to the group, is limited to self-employed farmers or "family employment." According to Nurkse also, "the term disguised unemployment is not applied to wage labor" (164, p. 33).

Some economists have, however, explained the coexistence of zero marginal productivity of hired worker and the positive wage rate, by making reference to non-economic considerations, like traditions and customs, that are said to enter into hiring practices. W. A. Lewis mentions some such practices prevailing in the underdeveloped countries:

Social prestige requires people to have servants, and the grand Seigneur may have to keep a whole army of retainers who are really little more than a burden upon his purse. This is not found only in domestic services, but in every sector employ- ment. Most businesses in underdeveloped countries employ a large number of "messengers" whose contribution is almost negligible; you see them sitting outside office doors, or hanging around in the courtyard. And even in the severest slump, the agricultural or commercial employer is expected to keep his labor force somehow or other....So it comes about that even in the sectors where people are working for wages and above all the domestic sector, marginal productivity may be negligible or even zero (130, p. 403).

M. L. Gupta (74) mentions the prevalence of Indian customs and ethical codes of behaviour that forbid the dismissal of workers from productive enterprises even if they are redundant. Describing labour conditions in Cuba, the International Bank for Recons- truction and Development mentioned in 1950 that it was difficult to dismiss a worker after he has been employed for six months (100). "Cultural and social practices like the patron-client relationship between land-owning families and labouring families, obligating the farmer to provide support to the latter," are according to Walter C. Neale (163, p. 167), crucial factors explaining zero mar- ginal productivity of farm workers coexisting with a positive wage rate. As for the labour-hiring practices in Japan, Alan H. Gleason mentions the social custom of treating an employee as a "mem- ber of the family," extending so far as "even to retain an unneeded or unsatisfactory worker" (71, p. 77). Tokutaro Yamanaka (274, p. 10) introduces the concept "family-labour-like" to indi- cate the position of the so-called wage labourers who are neither employed nor paid according to the mechanism of the economic calculus of equating the wage rate with the marginal revenue pro- duct of labour.

Such non-economic practices in hiring labour occur not only in the underdeveloped economies, but everywhere, including the most advanced industrial societies (e. g. the feather-bedding prac- tices enforced by collective bargaining contracts). The difference may be one of degree. In underdeveloped countries, these practi- ces are formalized into an overt social system and have become acceptable and expected procedures. The case of an entrepreneur, being guided by non-economic considerations in his hiring practices, is, in fact, analogous to the employment pattern in a joint family in an underdeveloped economy, where the existence of zero marginal product disguised unemployment is explained with reference to its social obligation to share "work and food" with its relatives. In our opinion, however, despite the non-economic behaviour entering into hiring of wage labourers and fixing their remuneration, generally, the employers, even in the agricultural sectors of underdeveloped economies, relate the real wage rate to the productivity of the hired labourer. This is evident from the variation in agricultural wages for men, women and children and also for different agricultural operations requiring different degrees of dexterity and skill. The Agricultural Labour Enquiry Committee (95, p. 117) found the following daily wage rates of adult male workers for various agricultural operations in India:

TABLE 1

DAILY WAGE RATES OF ADULT MALE
AGRICULTURAL WORKERS IN INDIA

Agricultural Operation	*Daily Wage Rates (Rupees)*	*Year*
Ploughing	1.05	1950-51
,,	1.00	1956-57
Weeding	0.89	1950-51
,,	0.88	1956-57
Transplanting	1.16	1950-51
,,	1.11	1956-57
Harvesting	1.26	1950-51
,,	0.93	1956-57

B. DISGUISED UNEMPLOYMENT WITH A SMALL POSITIVE MARGINAL
PHYSICAL PRODUCT IN THE STRICT STATIC SENSE

In this case, the marginal physical product of workers is actually positive, though small, in the strict static sense and their removal from farms would *per se* reduce total output. But this fall in output could be offset by modest increases in the quantity or quality of cooperating inputs or improvement in quality of labour inputs through:

(i) increased food intake of the remaining workers which raises

       productivity enough to restore output to the original level,[6]
- (ii) consolidation of small and fragmented pieces of land,
- (iii) changes in institutions, such as land tenure arrangements, which affect incentives and the distribution of agricultural income, and
- (iv) improvement in technical knowledge and increase or improvements in physical capital, such as tools, seeds, fertilizers or insecticides.

These changes would be tantamount to a shift in labour's marginal physical product curve, making it possible to remove some labour without decreasing the total output. It may be noted that the marginal physical product of disguised unemployed labour is positive in the strict static sense, but is zero in a loose dynamic sense.

THE THEORETICAL BASIS FOR A SMALL POSITIVE MARGINAL PHYSICAL PRODUCT IN THE STRICT STATIC SENSE

A small positive marginal physical product of labour can be explained in terms of utility maximizing behaviour which equates the utility added by the marginal product of labour with the marginal utility of leisure. For example, suppose that some workers operating the family farm are homogeneous in vigour and productivity and that the input of effective labour is uniform for each hour worked by any worker. The total and marginal physical product per worker for 5 workers and alternatively for 4 workers working on the family farm are shown in Table 2. The figures for the 5 workers' case are, of course, arbitrary, though internally consistent. Because we assume that the 5 workers are identical and that labour effort per hour is a constant, it follows that these figures are really derived from a function relating total product to total

[6]This assumption has also been made by Harvey Leibenstein (125) and Cho (31) in their analysis of the nature of disguised unemployment. The greater wage rate affords better consumption, which, in true, adds to the health, vigour and vitality of the average worker so that the work performed per unit of time is greater than that at lower income level. This assumption also implies that the economy will have to produce more food for feeding the workers removed from farms for employment on other projects. This would limit the use of surplus for capital formation as envisaged by Nurkse.

man-hours the identity of each worker being irrelevant. It follows in turn that, if one worker leaves the family, we can derive productivity figures for the 4-worker group from the same basic total output and total man-hour relationship. Thus, five workers putting in 8 hours per day for a total of 40 man-hours and four workers putting in 10 hours per day for the same total of 40 man-hours, both produce a total output of 290 units and the marginal product of the 40th man-hour is one unit.

Let us suppose in the five-worker case, that each of these workers has the same preference system and that each feels that the utility added by one unit of extra output from his eighth hour of work just equals the marginal utility of the sixteenth hour of leisure. Their total output will, therefore, be 290 units. Next, assume that one worker emigrates in search of better-paid work,[7] would the remaining four workers work for longer hours (10 hours each) so as to maintain the same total output of 290 units? For each of the four workers, the marginal utility of the sixteenth hour of leisure is unchanged. But his total product from 8 hours of work is now 59.75 units instead of 58 units. Depending on whether the income or substitution effect is stronger (assuming that leisure is not an inferior good), he may choose to work less or the same or more hours per day. However, we can be sure that he would not choose to work as much as 10 hours per day, for that would reduce the marginal physical product of the last man-hour of labour to one unit, as low as it was when each of the five workers chose to work an 8-hour day. This in turn would put the lower marginal utility of one last unit of output below the higher marginal utility of the 14th hour of leisure, so that this could not be an equilibrium. Therefore, total output would [definitely fall below two units which could only be attained if each of the four workers puts in a 10-hour day.

But the higher average real income of each of the four remaining workers will probably cause them to raise their food consumption,

---

[7] This assumption does not require recognition by workers of the availability of higher earning opportunities as a condition for their disguised unemployment. The main test for the existence of disguised unemployment lies in the size of the marginal product. The awareness on their part of the availability of opportunities of higher earning is, however, an important consideration for their removal to the urban centres.

TABLE 2

OUTPUT AND EMPLOYMENT ON FAMILY FARM

(1) Hours worked per worker per day	Five-worker case				Four-worker case			
	(2) Total product of each worker	(3) Marginal product of each man-hour	(4) Total product of 5 workers	(5) Marginal product of 5 man-hours	(6) Total product of each worker	(7) Marginal product of each man-hour	(8) Total product of 4 workers	(9) Marginal product of 4 man-hours
0	—	—	—	—	—	—	—	—
1	15.00	15.00	75.00	75.00	15.00	15.00	60.00	60.00
2	27.00	12.00	135.00	60.00	27.75	12.75	111.00	51.00
3	37.00	10.00	185.00	50.00	38.75	11.00	155.00	44.00
4	45.00	8.00	225.00	40.00	48.25	9.50	193.00	88.00
5	51.00	6.00	255.00	30.00	56.25	8.00	225.00	32.00
6	55.00	4.00	275.00	20.00	62.25	6.00	249.00	24.00
7	57.00	2.00	285.00	10.00	66.75	4.50	267.00	18.00
8	58.00	1.00	290.00	5.00	69.75	3.00	279.00	12.00
9	58.50	0.50	292.50	2.50	71.50	1.75	286.00	7.00
10	58.75	0.25	293.75	1.25	72.50	1.00	290.00	4.00

and if their productivity is an increasing function of their food intake, total production might rise enough to restore output to the original level. In this sense, the marginal physical product which was positive, though small, has been reduced to zero through improving the quality of the labour input. Strictly speaking, however, what has taken place is an upward *shift* of the function relating total product to total man-hour of labour.

C. DISGUISED UNEMPLOYMENT, WHERE THE MARGINAL PHYSICAL PRODUCT OF LABOUR IS SUBSTANTIALLY GREATER THAN ZERO, BUT LESS THAN THE REAL WAGE.

In the present case, however, the marginal physical product is positive (but less than the real wage rate) in the strict static sense and without fundamental dynamic changes as distinct from the modest changes mentioned in the previous section. Labour inputs cannot be withdrawn without substantially reducing the total output. According to N. K. Sarkar:

> Surplus labour exists if the value of marginal product is less than the rate of wage paid... the amount of surplus is to be measured by the excess of actual employment over the employment which equates marginal productivity and wage rate (218 p. 209).

Giving an economic interpretation of the concept of disguised unemployment, Bronfenbrenner remarks: "in economic terms, their marginal productivity is systematically below the level of food, shelter, pocket money or other income, paid them for their work (25). The literature on the subject may be discussed with respect to: (a) Family Farm Worker, (b) Hired Farm Labour, separately. The first category does not really require any further discussion beyond what has already been said.

1. DISGUISED UNEMPLOYMENT OF HIRED FARM LABOUR

In an earlier section of this chapter, while examining possible reasons for paying a positive wage rate to the hired farm worker with a zero marginal product, we found that most explanations offered were in terms of non-economic motivations, such as traditional and customary hiring practices. After examining these explanations, we concluded that while non-economic practices do occur, in general, employers do relate the real wage rate to the productivity of hired labour, even in the agricultural sectors of underdeveloped economies.

Some economists, however, have recently offered explanations rationalizing the employment of hired farm labour at a real wage rate greater than their marginal product.

Harvey Leibenstein (125-128) and Dipak Mazumdar (138) have provided one such explanation for agricultural wage rates greater than the marginal productivity of agricultural labour. These writers explain the phenomenon through the interaction between wage level, nutrition, and productivity. Assuming that workers spend their wage income on nutritional food and that their work effort is an increasing function of nutrition, the man-hours employed would vary directly with the level of wage rate. It would be in the interest of the landlord class as a whole to employ the entire labour force, through some institutional arrangement, leaving no pool of unemployed workers to drive wages down competitively to a lower level of nutrition. This may mean paying a real wage greater than their marginal product. This situation may be explained through the Leibenstein model shown in Fig. 2.11.

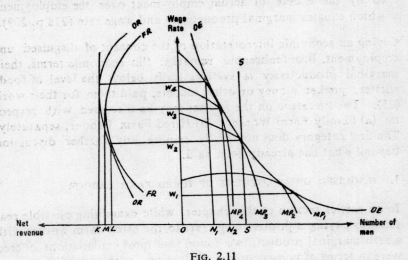

FIG. 2.11

On the right hand of Fig. 2.11, we have a family of marginal productivity curves. Each curve is related to a specific wage rate. MP_1-MP_4 indicate marginal productivity per man with wage rate W_1-W_4 respectively. The levels of these MP curves show that the higher the wage level, the greater is the marginal productivity of workers through interaction between wage level, nutrition, and productivity. The higher the wage rate, the more the consumption of nutritional foods and the greater the work effort. Points e_1-e_4 indicate the number of men the landlords would employ at the corresponding wage rates to maximize their income. Connecting all these points, we have a locus *OE* which is akin to the long-term demand curve for labour. *SS* is the related (inelastic) supply curve indicating that, in the short period, the supply of labour is approximately fixed. On the quadrant, on the left side of the diagram, the points on the optimum employment curve OE on the right side have been related to the net revenues obtained by landlords at various wage rates. For every wage rate and its optimum employment, there is a given net revenue to landlords as illustrated by the optimum employment revenue curve OR. For each MR, the net revenue is equal to the triangular area under the marginal productivity curve, above the wage line. If the entire labour force is employed, we obtain a full employment revenue curve FR. At some wage rates, the employment of the full labour force will involve employing a greater number of workers than the landlords wish to employ. At other wage rates, this will be too small to maximize their group income. In regard to the shape of OR and FR, at very low wage rate, the net revenue to landlords would be only slightly above zero. As wages increase, effort per man grows, optimum number of men declines, overhead cost per unit of work decreases, and, thus, the net revenue tends to rise. However, beyond a certain point, increase in wage rate increases work effort per man proportionately less than the wages. Hence, beyond some point, the higher the wage rate, the less the net revenue. For these reasons, the OR and FR curves are drawn U-shaped.

If landlords as a group were to maximize their net revenue, they would pay a wage of W_4 and hire ON_1 workers. At this wage rate, there will be excess supply of labour N_1S. But if there is nowhere for the surplus labour to go, competition among them would depress wages and wage rates would decline below the level W_4. It will eventually drop to OW_2, at which OE curve crosses the labour supply curve. But at this point, group net revenue drops to OL, (OL OK). From the FR curve, it would presumably be in the interest of the landlords (as a group) to employ the entire labour force, raise wages to OW_3 and enjoy a net revenue of $\underline{OM}$ OL. At the wage rate of OW_3 the landlords would utilize $\underline{ON_2}$ labour, while they would keep the entire labour force on the pay-roll, thus giving rise to the phenomenon of disguised unemployment. At OW_3 (and net revenue OM) there is disguised unemployment in the sense that the employment of the entire labour force results in the marginal product of labour smaller than its wage rate OW_3.

In this Leibenstein model, we should distinguish between the interests of the landlords as a group and as individuals. It was for group interest that the landlords, in the above model, were maximizing their total net revenue by employing all workers OS to maintain wage rate OW_3 greater than the marginal product. A single landlord, in his individual interest, would employ labourers so as to equate the wage rate with the latter's marginal product. This difference between the group and individual interests arises because an individual landlord is not in a position to hire all the labourers OS to maintain the wage rate at OW_3. Further, Leibenstein's theoretical model is based on an assumption of homogeneity of all agricultural workers in the matter of their skill and physical strength so that they are compensated approximately uniformly. It seems to assume that hardworking persons are not better rewarded. This view may be questioned, at least in respect of Asia. There is income differential between tenants and agricultural labourers with identical skill. The institution of leasing land to tenants is indirectly an attempt to compensate workers in proportion to changes in work effort and productivity, since the tenant receives a percentage share of the total produce. Furthermore, some employed farm workers are compensated on a piece basis, especially during harvest.

As already mentioned, the findings of the Indian Agricultural Enquiry Committee (95) show considerable variations in the range of daily wage rates for each group of unskilled workers. This also assumes landlordism (landlords owning land and agricultural labourers working for wages) as the land tenure system. In some underdeveloped countries, landlordism does not exist. In India, peasant proprietorship is the main land tenure arrangement; landlordism was abolished with the passage of

Zamindari Abolition Act in 1948-49. Moreover, Oshima (173) questions the figures of caloric intake and caloric requirement basic to the Leibenstein model. In his view there are no fixed standards of caloric requirements for good health. The standards differ for different purposes in different countries, depending on climatic and physical characteristics of the population. Accordingly, Oshima remarks, "for purposes of Leibenstein theory, food requirements may have to be established for each country and standardized for each type of occupation and season of the year" (173). Leibenstein's theory of employment in backward economies is valuable in emphasizing the relation between wage income, nutrition level, intensity of work effort and the level of employment. It lacks relevance to the actual conditions obtaining in India, especially as regards the land tenure system.

CHAPTER THREE

DISGUISED UNEMLPOYMENT AND THE DEVELOPMENT OF THE DUAL ECONOMY

SOME WRITERS have recently tried to relate disguised unemployment to the stages of development by which a dual economy—with a family firm sector and hired labour sector—is gradually converted into an exclusively hired labour economy.

We may start with W. A. Lewis (130) who laid the groundwork of the idea. He developed a model of an economy with a subsistence (rural) sector and capitalistic (urban) sector, with surplus labour available in both. In the urban sector, surplus labour may be openly unemployed. In the rural sector, surplus labour is disguised in the sense that everyone is working but if some portion is withdrawn, total output will not fall. In the rural sector, a farm worker, as a member of a joint family, receives his average product (real wage rate), not his own marginal product. Unless there is an opportunity for earning a real wage greater than this average product, there is no motivation to leave the farm for employment elsewhere. This average product per worker in agriculture determines the "traditional wage." This "traditional wage," in the subsistence rural sector, sets a floor to wages in the capitalistic sector. This wage level remains unchanged until the surplus labour in the subsistence (rural) sector is eliminated. This model, however, has its minor shortcomings. Lewis does not take into consideration adequately the cultural and social factors affecting the transference of surplus rural labour to the urban industrial sector. We will discuss this factor in more detail later. Furthermore, while it is true that the surplus farm worker would not move to the capitalist urban sector unless he is paid a real wage higher than his average earnings in the family, he might be quite happy to work on public projects in his own village at less than the "traditional wage" to supplement earnings of the family that he would continue to enjoy anyway. In fact, if the surplus worker migrates from home, the welfare of remaining members would be improved by their higher average real incomes. Therefore, they might agree to pay to the departing member a part of his share in the family's earnings. In such a case, the worker might accept an income lower than the "traditional wage" to work elsewhere. But these reservations do not alter the main conclusion reached by Lewis.

Further, elaborations and amendments have been made in the Lewis model by Gustav Ranis and John C. Fei (198, 199) and by Stephen Enke (60). Lewis model of economic development with unlimited supplies of labour, according to Ranis and Fei (199), explains the expansion of the capitalistic industrial sector, nourished by supplies of cheap labour from the subsistence agricultural sector. But it fails to present a satisfactory analysis of changes in the subsistence sector itself. They have traced the following three phases of development of the agricultural sector. (1) Zero marginal productivity—labour—the redundant labour could be transferred from agriculture without decreasing total output. (2) The marginal product of labour then becomes positive, but is still less than the institutional wage rate. There is disguised unemployment—in a recent publication Fei and Ranis (199) have used the term "non-redundant labour" in place of disguised unemployment—but the agricultural manpower could not be withdrawn without decrease in total output. (3) The equalization of the marginal product and the real wage in agriculture. This final stage marks the commercialization of agriculture, the institutional wage is abandoned and disguised unemployment disappears. These three stages are shown in Figs. 3.1 and 3.2.

In Fig. 3.1, labour is measured on the horizontal axis, and marginal and average products on the vertical axis. If OA is the total labour force in agriculture, its marginal product is zero. Since the total agricultural output is consumed by OA labour, the share of each (real wage) will be equal to AS. The persistence of this wage level (institutional wage rate) is sustained by institutions like the joint family system, since otherwise, under competitive assumptions, the real wage would fall to zero. The institutional wage AS in the agricultural sector would also become the basic wage rate in the industrial sector. At this institutional wage rate, OG would be the optimum amount of labour to be hired in agriculture under the competitive conditions. Labour represented by AG is thus disguised unemployed, since their marginal product is less than the wage rate AS. This disguised unemployed labour would move to the industrial capitalistic sector gradually. In Fig.

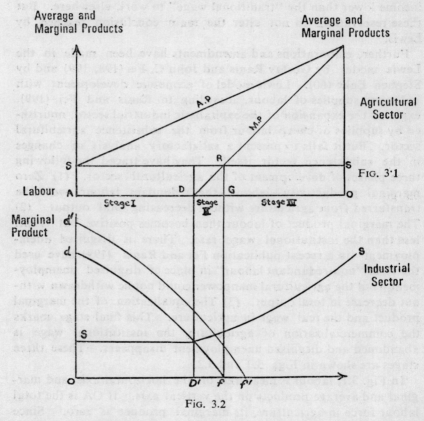

FIG. 3·1

Fig. 3.2

3.2, labour and the marginal product are measured on the horizontal and vertical axes respectively. AD in Fig. 3.1 and OD in Fig. 3.2 mark Stage 1. The marginal product is zero and during this stage AD (or less) labour can be withdrawn from agriculture without diminishing total output. In Fig. 3.2, Stage 1 conforms to Lewis' unlimited labour supply curve with d'f' as the demand curve for labour in industry.

During Stage II (in Fig. 3.1), the marginal product of labour is positive but less than the wage rate AS. DG labour cannot be withdrawn without reducing agricultural output somewhat. In Fig. 3.2, with additional capital investment, the demand curve for labour would shift to the right up to d'f'. But since the labour supply curve SS in the industrial sector has started rising during Stage II, the period of unlimited labour supply would end.

During Stage III, the marginal product of labour will eventually become equal to the wage rate AS. The disguised unemployment will end and we have the commercialization of agriculture. At this stage, the institutional wage is passed and competitive market forces yield an equilibrium level of employment OG in Fig. 3.1. The contribution of Ranis and Fei lies in looking at the disguised unemployment in agriculture from this dynamic point of view.

A. REMOVAL OF THE DISGUISED UNEMPLOYED LABOUR— SOCIAL AND CULTURAL INSTITUTIONS

In this section we shall discuss the role of social and cultural institutions of an underdeveloped economy in connection with the removal of disguised unemployed labour for utilization in the economic development process.

In the literature on economic development, the existence of disguised unemployment in the agricultural sector of underdeveloped economies has been viewed as an asset for industrialization, or in the words of W.A. Lewis, "a source of capital formation at zero cost in other goods" (130. p. 218). In estimating rural disguised unemployment, economists have assumed that all, or most, of this surplus labour could be removed from the farms without diminishing the total farm output. But since in an underdeveloped economy these unemployed workers are members of a joint family that shares its work and real income (including psychic income), they would need some inducement to leave their homes and hearths. According to Navarretes, "The process of shifting labor units from a position of underemployment to more productive activities requires the incentives of higher rewards" (162, p. 236). They do not, however, specify the nature of such reward. W. Arthur

Lewis elaborated on this point:

> ...the minimum at which labor can be had is now set by the average product of the farmer; the men will not leave the family farm to seek employment if the wage is worth less than they would be able to consume if they remained at home (130, p. 409).

Lewis recognized the existence of several institutional factors that would necessitate paying a real wage greater than the real income consumed by the worker when living with his family. According to Lewis:

> Earnings in the subsistence sector set a floor to wages in the capitalist sector, but in practice wages have to be higher than this and there is usually a gap of 30 per cent or more between capitalist wages and subsistence earnings....This may be required because of the psychological cost of transferring from the easy to the more regimented and urbanized environments of the capitalist sector (130, p. 411).

While Lewis estimated that a 30 per cent margin would induce the unemployed worker to emigrate from his rural environment, according to Fei and Ranis:

> ...the land tenure system, the extended family structure, the social consensus with respect to a given community's obligation to individual welfare—the dominance, in short, of the entire non-economic nexus of mores and relationships which determine income distribution in the agricultural sector of the underdeveloped economy...(199, p. 21), do not lend themselves readily to a rigorous measure of the exact magnitude of the real agricultural wage in any particular country.

In the circumstances, again according to Fei and Ranis: "....It is even more difficult to attempt any generalization of such determination with applicability to all labour surplus underdeveloped countries" (199, p. 22).

In view of these difficulties, they take average productivity of rural workers as the "institutional wage rate" in the model outlined in the previous section. Young Sam Cho, analyzing the nature of disguised unemployment in underdeveloped areas, emphasizes cultural and traditional institutions, such as the joint family-clan village system which, "give both farm owning and non-farm owning family members a sense of belonging, mutual trust, a non-disciplined life and peace of mind" (31, p. 35). The phenomenon of disguised unemployment, according to Cho, represents a conscious choice of an individual to live with his family though underemployed and leading:

> ...a miserable life, ridden by hunger and disease....The people living in impoverished rural communities are, of course, economically not happy, but neither are they unhappy enough to break through the traditional social institutions (31, pp. 140-1).

Cho characterizes the phenomenon as "tradition-directed underemployment" and its being voluntary is "not withdrawable from the land without a social change and/or changes in the economy such as the attraction of substantially higher earnings in alternative occupations" (31, p. 141). How high should be these earnings in the alternative occupations? No generalization, according to Cho, could be made on this question, since "labour that may be available in one society at a particular wage may not ibe available at the same wage in other societies" (31, p. 45).

In connection with the removability of farm workers, Cho speaks of two personality groups—"socially marginal" and "economically marginal," individuals. A socially marginal individual is one:

> who leaves one social or economic group without making a satisfactory adjustment to enter another, finds himself on the margin of each but a member of neither....Because of his uncertain position from a social or economic point of view, he is not particularly likely to try to make new adjustments in situations of change (31, p. 32).

Cho's second personality type is the "economically marginal" individual who, in poor peasant farming, is found:

> poised in ambivalence between the desire for a higher material scale of living in some distant industrial area and the material

conditions of the life they know. In the presence of this apparent conflict, these people are especially likely to make new adjustments whenever a change in the economic structure occurs (31, p. 33).

The "socially marginal" are most likely to be "economically marginal" but the reverse may not be true. Using this classification, the simultaneously "socially and economically marginal individual," is withdrawable (even away from his village), while the economically (but not socially) marginal individual is not withdrawable but could be mobilized for work on projects near his own village. Cho's main contribution lies in relating disguised unemployment in a traditional underdeveloped economy with people's attitudes towards social and cultural values of life. In studying the worker's occupational preferences, we must not ignore their social and cultural traditions. But these non-economic aspects cannot always be easily quantified—an essential part of economic development planning. While discussing the utilization of surplus labour, Cho recognizes the weakness of his concept of "tradition-directed" idle labour from an operational point of view. The notion of "social changes," which would make the tradition-directed disguised unemployed workers withdrawable, is also rather elusive.

We tend to agree with Fei and Ranis, and with Cho, that no generalization could be made on the nature and amount of inducements attractive enough to make the disguised unemployed workers emigrate from their families and communities. Not only, as Cho suggests, would each society differ on this issue, but, even within the same society, the question of necessary inducements of removal of surplus labour would depend on the type of households on the bases of their castes, customs, and traditions. To consider the effect of these social and cultural institutions, we can divide rural households in an underdeveloped economy into the following categories:

(i) The households whose members would like to supplement their income, but are not willing to work as wage earners. Members of very high castes, descendants of old ruling families or landlords would not like to bring shame on the names of their families by reducing themselves to the position of low status or low-caste wage earners. No reasonable amount of monetary inducement would make them leave their families. Such families are negligible in number. To provide more work for them, it might be possible to furnish them with financial aid and technical know-how to start small industries or trade. Some of these households might be considered voluntarily unemployed and excluded from the labour force.

(ii) Families whose underemployed members are willing (even at a rate lower than their share in family income, which they would continue to consume) to accept jobs for wages on local projects (construction of buildings, irrigation and flood control projects, roads, etc.). Their traditional family ties are so strong, however, that the members do not wish to leave their families and villages, even temporarily, in order to migrate to urban centres to find work.

(iii) Households whose members, in their anxiety to supplement the family income, are ready to move to nearby urban centres and work in seasonal industries without much inducement, i.e. at a real wage rate equal to their share in the family's income. They are not, however, willing to leave their joint families permanently without a substantial increase in their real wage, since their services are needed in agricultural operations during the peak agricultural season and their emotional and psychological attachments to their families are quite strong. Even while these members are away at work, they keep up their strong association with the joint family in various ways. Thus, a man may leave his wife and children with the extended family and he would place his earnings at the disposal of the family head. In this category we find cultivating tenants and agricultural labourers with some land of their own, especially in the Asian rural societies.

(iv) Families which do not have any attachment to the land as owners or tenants and which are just living in the villages of their ancestors. These households generally belong to the lowest rung of the social ladder. They have no scruples about accepting certain jobs. While in the village, they offer themselves for wages to the landowners as casual or attached workers. If there is no work in the village, they would not hesitate to migrate to other rural or urban areas to find work within the range of their skills on, either a temporary or permanent basis and without much increase in their present real wage rate. In most underdeveloped countries, such agricultural wage labour provides manpower for seasonal industries in urban areas, plantations and in the mining operations. Their unemployment is open rather than disguised. In this case, either a worker is unemployed or actively looking for work.

For the purpose of classifying households in the above categories, the following are some of the useful indicators:

(i) The ratio of dependants (other than minor children) to the earning members; the higher the ratio, the more tradition-bound the society will be. The underemployed members of such a society will be less mobile in moving outside their villages in search of work, and higher inducement will have to be offered to move them elsewhere for utilization.

(ii) The general level of education, especially western style education of the household; generally speaking, the higher the level of education, the lesser the impact of customs and tradition on work attitudes.

(iii) The nature of the religious and cultural beliefs; religious beliefs usually affect the nature of economic activity. Some religions teach that salvation or spiritual fulfilment is found in meditation and renunciation. Others teach that it is found also, or alternatively, in work. It is, however, difficult to decide how much importance to attribute to religion in economic matters.

B. NATURE OF THE POLITICAL AND ECONOMIC SYSTEM

In connection with the removal of disguised unemployed for utilization elsewhere, it is also important to take into account the nature of the political and economic system of the society under consideration. Though there are various shades of political systems from "socialism" to "democratic socialism," and from "laissez-faire" capitalism to "guided democracy," we shall take into consideration a socialistic system in which the means of production are owned by the State (Government or "Commune") and the workers have no choice in selecting the duration and place of work. By compelling workers to put in more time at the same real wage rate, a socialist government can easily render a part of the surplus rural work force for use elsewhere, as shown in Figs. 3.3 and 3.4.

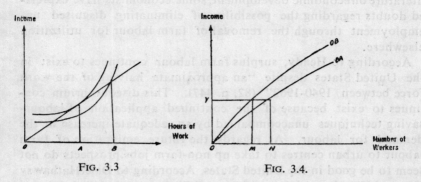

FIG. 3.3   FIG. 3.4.

Fig. 3.3 shows the relationship between income and effort yielded by the indifference map of a typical worker. Given a free choice between effort and leisure, he would put in OA effort. In Fig. 3.4, we have a corresponding production function OA with ON worker producing OY total output. With a view to withdrawing some workers from agriculture, the government can compel each worker to increase his effort (reduce his leisure) from OA to OB without increasing the wage rate. In Fig. 3.4, the production function will shift upward to the position OB. It will be noted that the number of workers required to produce OY output has been reduced from ON to OM, rendering MN workers surplus for removal from the land.

It was through this technique of compulsion that the Soviet Government could secure a large number of farm workers for industrialization. On the other hand, in a capitalist system (also synonymous with "free society," democracy," etc.) the means of production are owned by the households and they make their own decision about the duration and place of work. Except in emergencies like war, the individual is not forced to work against his will.

C. POSSIBILITY AND DESIRABILITY OF ELIMINATING DISGUISED UN-EMPLOYMENT THROUGH EMIGRATION FROM THE RURAL SECTOR

While on the one hand, the removal of disguised unemployment from the rural areas has been receiving increasing attention in the

literature on economic development, some economists have express-
ed doubts regarding the possibility of eliminating disguised unemployment through the removal of farm labour for utilization
elsewhere.

According to Heady, surplus farm labour continues to exist in
the United States despite "an approximate halving of the work
force between 1940-1962" (82, p. 447). This disequilibrium continues to exist because of the continued application of labour-
saving techniques unaccompanied by an adequate increase in the
demand for labour. As regards the future emigration of farm
labour to urban centres to take up non-farm jobs, prospects do not
seem to be good in the United States. According to Dale Hathaway
(80, p. 365), those jobs (either unskilled or semi-skilled labour)
promise to show the greatest relative decline or smallest absolute
growth over the coming decade because of the progress of auto-
mation in the economy. American agriculture will thus continue
to face the problem of excess labour supply and the resultant low
incomes, unless aggregate demand in the economy is expanded
sufficiently to provide full employment. The mere emigration of
farm labour is not likely to completely solve the problem of
disguised unemployment in the American rural sector.

Some economists doubt the desirability of encouraging the
emigration of farm workers to urban centres because of the problems of adjustments to the urban way of life and the adverse
effect of emigration on the rural communities. Lyle Shannon
mentions the problems of adjustments of urban migrants from
rural communities in the United States:

> ...the farm-reared are over-represented in low status positions,
> whether the measure of status is education, occupation, family
> income, or self-perception of status. The farm-reared held low
> status jobs and earned low incomes. These findings remained
> even when age, sex, color, and region of present residence were
> held constant (227, p. 123).

According to Carl Eicher and Lawrence Witt, "Migration often
results in so many new urban dwellers that some must live in
shipping crates or metal shacks in urban slums (58, p. 205). These
adjustment problems involved in the transfer of rural labour to

the urban areas have brought this reaction from the Farmers' Union: "Emphasis on training low-income people to leave farming is a negative approach" (80, p. 379).

Philip Raup (202) has pointed out the social costs involved in the emigration from the rural communities, in the shape of declining community facilities, such as schools and churches. According to Raup, there are economies of scale in rural service centres and he lists some requirements for a rural community to remain viable: (1) a supply area adequate to provide a sufficient volume of farm products necessary to enable the efficient operation of processing and assembly functions; (2) a trade territory large enough to support the provisions of producers' supplies and services at the minimum cost; (3) an internal labour market large enough to provide a range of job opportunities sufficient to effectively utilize the local labour force; and (4) a tax base and economic structure sufficient to support an adequate structure of community services, such as schools, churches, and public utilities. With the decline in the rural population, these requirements are not met with the resultant deterioration of small towns and inadequate services such as banking and credit, machinery maintenance and repair, medical care and education, and public utilities. These public costs associated with the decline of rural communities should be taken into account when formulating policies for the removal of farm labour to solve the problem of disguised unemployment.

The problems raised by the emigration or rural manpower in the United States apply equally to the conditions in the underdeveloped countries. Due to the preponderance of the rural sector in these economies, the size of the industrial labour force is almost trivial relative to the number of persons engaged in agriculture. The growth of facilities in the urban sector has not been able to keep pace with the increasing urban population. Emigration from the rural sector accentuates the overcrowding, slums, and insanitary conditions. Furthermore, in the overcrowded cities in the underdeveloped countries, underemployment and unemployment are already quite large. According to the Planning Commission of India (93), 28 per cent of the families in Calcutta were affected by unemployment in 1953. In the circumstances, it would, perhaps, be a mistake to move people from rural areas into urban areas in India. The best way to solve the problem of disguised unemployment, according to the Planning Commission of India, would be to start comprehensive work programmes in each rural area:

> where many projects are calling for considerable amounts of unskilled and skilled labour, e.g. irrigation and flood control projects, land reclamation schemes including water-logging and drainage and the reclamation of saline lands, afforestation and soil conservation schemes, roads, etc. (97, p. 2).

CHAPTER FOUR

MEASUREMENT OF DISGUISED UNEMPLOY-
MENT—A SURVEY OF MEASUREMENT
TECHNIQUES

SCANNING THE voluminous literature on measurement of disguised unemployment, we can categorize most of the methods employed into: (a) Direct method, and (b) Indirect method. The direct method of measurement, also known as "survey method," is based on an empirical sample inquiry by questionnaire to ascertain directly from the households, information on the extent of labour utilization, i.e. labour actually used as a proportion of total labour, the households are willing and able to supply. In the indirect method, also referred to as "norm method" or "secondary data approach," information on the extent of labour utilization is obtained from secondary data, such as publications from government and other research organizations. The various measurement techniques are listed below:

DIRECT METHOD

TIME-WORKED NORM

Labour Force Approach. The employment status of a worker is classified on the basis of his actual economic activity. To ascertain, from households directly, the labour time the workers are actually working in the various agricultural operations as a proportion of the labour time, they are willing and able to work (Fernando Sierra Berdecia and A.J. Jaffe (10), Orlando (172), Indian Sample Survey (96), Japanese Labour Survey (110), Puerto Rican Labour Survey (191, 192).

Gainful Worker Approach. To ascertain from households the number of labour units the workers are actually putting in various agricultural operations as a proportion of the labour units required to maintain the present farm output.

The following are the criteria suggested to estimate the amount of labour units required in the above case. (a) The family farm worker should put in labour time equivalent to labour time put in by farm wage labourers (Young Sam Cho (31); (b) the optimum labour time required for the existing total farm output on the area with existing techniques of cultivation and capital investment. Optimum labour time implies the minimum labour time for the given level of output. For determining the optimum labour time, the following methods have been used:

(i) Production function method—fitting a regression line and maximizing total output with respect to labour input (John W. Mellor, 140).

(ii) Labour time required is estimated for different agricultural operations from information collected in sampling inquiries distinguishing between different types of cultivation and different sizes and forms of land tenure (P. N. Rosenstein-Rodan, 210, 211).

(iii) Labour required on family farms is estimated on the basis of employment pattern of workers on the well-managed farms, Netherlands Agricultural Economic Research Institute (122).

Work and Income Norm. To ascertain from rural households the amount of land they are actually cultivating and the size of land they would be willing and able to cultivate with the existing capital, including livestock and labour input. The difference between these indicates the extent of underemployment (Mujumdar, 156).

INDIRECT METHOD OF MEASUREMENT

TIME-WORKED NORM

Labour Available on the Farms. From the census and occupational surveys, the number of workers in the farm work force is determined by standardizing men, women and children into homo-geneous units on the basis of prevailing wage rates. The number of homogeneous labour units is multiplied by a "labour-time-avail-able" norm to compute the total number of labour days available in the reference period (usually a year) in the area. The "labour-time-available" norm is based on the following criteria:

(a) Number of working days in a year and number of working hours per day fixed by government in the minimum Agri-cultural Wages Act.

(b) Decision by the persons in charge of the inquiry on the number of man-days per month or year a worker should work, taking into account the number of national and religious holidays and man-days lost due to climatic factors.

Labour Required. Labour time required to produce the existing total agricultural output, or to cultivate the total area under culti-vation, is estimated through formulating a norm of "labour time required." The norm is fixed on the following criteria (with given techniques of cultivation, farm management practices, including size and distribution of landholdings, level of capital investment and the social economic and cultural patterns of rural house-holds):

(a) The labour time needed to farm a unit of land area for growing various crops and to handle a number of cattle and other agricultural operations (M. Srinivasan, 241; Hoon K. Lee, 124; United Nations Economic Commission for Europe, 259; John Lossing Buck, 26).

(b) The labour time required to produce units of different crops and other farm products, e.g. labour time needed to produce 100 pounds of wheat, etc. (Greek Labour Survey 186).

For determining the labour coefficients, average of labour/land and labour/output ratios for farming in the area serve as a basis. These labour coefficients are based on the results of sample surveys of farms in the several regions of the country producing different crops and under different patterns of cultivation.

Work and Income Norm. Size of land necessary to provide an average family with full employment is decided upon and called "optimum" or "economic" holding. The difference between the area actually cultivated and the size of "optimum holding" would indicate the extent of underemployment (Tarlok Singh, 235; Doreen Warriner, 265; M. L. Gupta, 74).

OTHER METHODS OF MEASURING DISGUISED UNEMPLOYMENT

The ratio between the density of population deemed adequate— "standard rural density"—for the existing farm conditions and the actual density of population prevailing in that area indicate the level of disguised unemployment (Doreen Warriner, 265).

We have mentioned above in bare outlines various methods that have been used to estimate the extent of disguised unemployment in agriculture. We shall now explain and examine some of these methods from the point of view of their usefulness in measuring the extent of this phenomenon in the rural sector of an underdeveloped economy. We shall take at least one method from each category for critical evaluation.

I. DIRECT METHOD OF ESTIMATING DISGUISED UNEMPLOYMENT

IA. LABOUR FORCE APPROACH—TIME-WORKED NORM

We shall now outline and examine some surveys using the labour force approach, which are conducted regularly in Japan, India and Puerto Rico to estimate the level of unemployment. In these surveys, a sample of households are interviewed to obtain information on the level of employment—how many hours (or days) per week they are actually working and the number of hours they would want to work. The worker's own judgment on his level of work activity and his requirement for additional work are the bases for his classification as employed or unemployed. Emphasis is placed on the worker's willingness and ability to work in classifying his employment level.

IA (1). NATIONAL SAMPLE SURVEY—REPORT ON EMPLOYMENT AND UNEMPLOYMENT IN INDIA

National Sample Survey, started by the Indian Statistical Institute in 1950-51, has become a regular source of statistics on the economic and social aspects of national life. It is now conducted twice a year. The survey is national in scope and covers both rural and urban areas. The unit is a household, defined as "a community of persons living together and eating at the same board for a period of 16 days or more during the 30 days preceding the survey." The survey makes use of a detailed questionnaire covering extremely wide fields: consumption and production (agricultural and industrial), transportation, employment, unemployment financial services, housing, education, prices, wages, etc. The sample and questionnaire are changed from time to time to meet any specific need.

The first comprehensive survey, as a part of the National Sample Survey to collect information on the extent and character of rural employment and unemployment on the national level, was undertaken between the period May-November 1955. The size of the sample was 16,240 households spread all over India. Information was gathered about the daily particulars of economic activity during the seven days preceding the day of enquiry; (a) hours at work, (b) hours available for work.

On the basis of this information, the labour force was classified into categories of employed, unemployed and the underemployed as explained below:

(a) *Employed and Unemployed.* A person is regarded as employed or unemployed with reference to his current status during the enumeration period. A person reporting his status as having "gainful work" has been treated as employed, while a person reporting "seeking work" has been classified as unemployed. Of the total rural workers, 0.41 per cent were found to be unemployed in the survey (96).

(b) *Underemployed.* This has been referred to as the underutilization of manpower. Its magnitude is measured as a difference between the weekly hours actually at work and the number of hours available (able and willing) to work. In order to arrive at a definite estimate of underemployment, a norm of full employment (43 to 56 hours per week or 6 to 8 hours per day) has been used. On the basis of the information on "actual employment" and "desired employment" the results of the survey are as follows.

Persons working for 28 hours or less a week or on an average of four hours or less a day and available for extra work constitute 8.8 per cent of the gainfully employed in rural areas. On the assumption that 43 to 56 hours a week is the general norm of full employment in India, these are deemed "severely underemployed." Persons working for 29 to 56 hours a week or more (four hours and up to eight hours a day on an average) and available for extra work come to 5.51 per cent of the rural work force (96, p. 14).

According to these findings, the main employment problem in the Indian rural economy is that of underemployment, rather than unemployment proper.

IA (2). THE ITALIAN 1952 SURVEY

In December 1951, the Italian Chamber of Deputies ordered a comprehensive inquiry into the   characteristics and causes of underemployment in relation to several economic and social factors in Italy (253). The scope of the survey specifically included an assessment of agricultural underemployment in   certain   large farming areas of the country. In the survey, both interview and questionnaire techniques were used to collect information on the number of man-days available and man-days actually worked from a sample covering 98 large farm holdings and 176 farm families.

To estimate the number of man-days available, a distinction was drawn between different forms of work performed by each member of a family; e.g. wage earning jobs for an employer or agricultural work on family holdings. The information was tabulated separately for men and women between the ages of 18 and 65, for children, and for persons over the age of 65. To express the total labour time available in some homogeneous units (adult man-hours) the time available by women was given a weight of 0.60 and that by children and persons over the age of 65 a weight of 0.50. The number of working days in a year was fixed in regard to local farming practices, care of livestock, transportation to the place of work, the need of ancillary industries, supervision and miscellaneous maintenance jobs. Housework done by women at home was counted as an economic activity. The number of working hours available was calculated on the following basis:

(i) Three hundred working days a year for men and women, working in the fields and 360 days a year for women employed exclusively on household work.

(ii) nine hours a day for share-croppers, eight hours a day for wage-earners and nine hours a day for women engaged in house-work.

The total number of man-days actually worked were collected directly from the households and tables were drawn for each region of the country and for different types of land tenures. The figures were further broken down by seasons to bring about seasonal fluctuations in the level of employment. After estimating the man-days available and number of man-days actually worked, the extent of underemployment was found by comparing these statistics. The Committee found that the "Italian agricultural workers are without work for 94 days or 34 per cent of 270 to 280 days available in a year" (253, p. 269). According to the Committee, "these figures indicate that one of the most conspicuous outward signs of labour inactivity in Italy was pronounced underemployment of almost half the total labour force of the nation" (253, p. 269).

IA (3). SURVEY OF RURAL UNEMPLOYMENT IN PUNJAB (INDIA)

With a view to assessing the extent and form of unemployment and underemployment in the rural areas of Punjab (India), the Board of Economic Enquiry, Punjab (194) conducted a survey of employment conditions in rural areas during the period October-December 1955. The scope of the survey was restricted to the rural areas of Jullundur and Karnal Districts, which are fairly representative of the two regions of the state. In all, 1198 households were contacted and the following information on the employment level was obtained by interviewing the heads of the households:

(i) Activity status of members:

(a) Employed (in gainful activity on any day during the reference period).

(b) Unemployed (without a job for the whole of the month of reference period, was seeking a job and was able to accept a job if offered).

(c) Not in the labour force—categories (a) and (b) plus those not seeking employment but available for work constitute the labour force. Persons other than those included in the labour force were classified as "not in the labour force," like family members engaged in household and domestic work, voluntarily unemployed, e.g. rentiers, pensioners, etc., children, the infirm and students.

(d) Underemployed (number of months actually worked in a year).

For information on employment and underemployment, the reference period was the month preceding the date of interview. To find the extent of underemployment, employment particulars for the previous year were recorded and the intensity of employment was measured in months per year.

The findings of the survey are mentioned below:

(i) Unemployed	2.81 per cent of the total rural population
(ii) Employed	32.19 per cent of the total rural population
(iii) Not in labour force	65.00 per cent of the total rural population
(iv) Underemployment (intensity of employment)	See Table 3

About 58 per cent of all employed persons remain busy in agricultural operations from 9 to 12 months in a year. According to the survey, these may fairly be treated as fully employed. Of the other 42 per cent, 10 per cent are employed for less than 6 months (severely underemployed) and about 33 per cent are busy for about 7 to 9 months (underemployed) in a year.

IA (4). THE PUERTO RICAN LABOUR SURVEY

The Bureau of Labour Statistics of the Puerto Rico Department of Labour (191,192) has been conducting labour force surveys throughout the country to obtain statistics on employment patterns of the working populations as well as the general economic and social conditions of the labour force. In 1952, the scope of the

TABLE 3

PERCENTAGE DISTRIBUTION OF EMPLOYED PERSONS
(CULTIVATORS ONLY) BY NUMBER OF MONTHS
EMPLOYED IN THE PREVIOUS YEAR

Employment in the year (in months)	Total
1- 3	—
3- 6	1.59
6- 7	8.05
7- 8	5.59
8- 9	26.80
9-10	22.02
10-11	22.18
11-12	13.67

labour survey was extended to elicit information on the extent of underemployment which, according to the Bureau of Labour is a serious problem in Puerto Rico. The universe is all persons aged 14 and above, and the sample included 13,000 households. The survey is conducted quarterly and the reference period is the week preceding the date when enumerators interview the respondents. The labour force in Puerto Rico is classified in the following categories:

(i) *Labour Force* comprising the civilian non-institutional population, 14 years of age and over.
(ii) *Employed* persons who during the survey were either:
    (a) at work—those who worked for pay or profit or worked without pay for 15 hours or more on a family farm, or
    (b) with a job but not at work.
(iii) *Unemployed* persons who did not work at all during the week and were actually looking for work.
(iv) *Underemployed*
    (a) *Visible Underemployment*—employees who worked for less than 35 hours and also looked for additional work.
    (b) *Invisible or Disguised Unemployment*—those self-employed and unpaid family workers, and
    (c) who were engaged in subsistence or semi-subsistence,

farming, i.e. they consumed rather than sold a major part of their produce.

It will be observed that the self-employed and unpaid family workers have been accorded a special treatment in this survey. The survey report remarks: "In Puerto Rico, observations confirm that subsistence or quasi-subsistence farm workers suffer from invisible underemployment. They produce little, i.e. have low level of productivity" (191, 192). Accordingly, all self-employed and unpaid family workers engaged in subsistence agriculture are classified as underemployed and no specific estimate about the extent of their disguised unemployment is made. The Puerto Rican Survey is not very helpful as a method of measuring the extent of agricultural underemployment, since our objective in this study is not merely to ascertain the existence of the phenomenon, but to measure its extent. The Puerto Rican criterion of characterizing a farm household as underemployed simply, because it consumes a major part of its produce, can lead to misleading results. For example, during the depression when the prices of agricultural commodities fall, the small farmers have to sell a large part of their meagre agricultural output to meet expenses on fixed obligations like land revenue and other taxes, debt instalments, and interest. According to the Puerto Rican criterion, these households would be fully employed, as they are selling the major part of their produce. But, in fact, these households would be in a state of underemployment and extreme distress. This test, is, thus unreliable for measuring the extent of disguised unemployment.

IA (5). EVALUATION OF LABOUR FORCE APPROACH—TIME-WORKED NORM

An important feature of the survey using the worker's willingness and availability to work in classifying his level of employment, is the recognition of his preference work and leisure. It is argued that to question the productiveness or usefulness of a worker's effort is tantamount to challenging the rationality of his behaviour. If the individual acting in his self-interest knows what is best for him, we have no basis to pronounce judgement on the productiveness of his effort. In the circumstances, it is asserted that we should not consider any person as unemployed or under-employed before asking him specifically whether or not he is willing and able to work.

We have already discussed disguised underemployment with reference to preference between work and leisure and were of the opinion that, what seems to be leisure, is often enforced idleness resulting from lack of the cooperating inputs like land and capital. Furthermore, to rely on workers' ability to indicate the number of hours they would like to work, is to assume that they are urban industrial workers, for whom it is not very difficult to decide whether they wish to obtain extra work. Even if they are not actively looking for work they are nevertheless perfectly clear in their own minds whether or not they are ready to undertake any extra work or full-time job, that may arise. When asked if they wish to work full time, they can usually give a clear answer which permits classifying them without ambiguity. This is not true of the self-employed in general and of family farm workers in underdeveloped countries in particular. Unpaid family workers have difficulty in stating their share in operating the family farm. Moreover, when dealing with a wage-earning population or people who are fully accustomed to monetary forms of economy, a statement that an individual wishes to obtain more or better-paid work can be reasonably used as a criterion for the purpose of classifying him as underemployed. On the other hand, when a survey is conducted among a non-wage-earning population which has only a slight acquaintance with a monetary economy and where (due to the institution of joint family system) there is no relation between work effort and share in family earnings, it is highly doubtful whether questions about willingness to obtain more or less paid work are likely to elicit worthwhile replies. It is not possible to place much reliance on this largely subjective procedure.

A worker, who is aware of the number of hours (or days) he is actually working and the number of hours he would be willing to work, is a visibly underemployed person, while in the underdeveloped rural societies, the underemployment is mostly in an invisible or disguised form. Another limitation from which this "labour survey approach" suffers is that these surveys are conducted only once or twice a year, and the information regarding the hours of work actually put in during the reference period may not represent the year-round work position.   These surveys thus give us information on seasonal rather than on the chronic aspect of underemployment that we intend to measure.   Because of the serious shortcomings in the "labour survey method," all the subsistence farm workers in Puerto Rican labour survey have been treated as underemployed.   These problems make it necessary to adopt some more objective criteria to estimate the difference between the amount of labour inputs actually being used on the farms and that are required to maintain the existing level of output.

I-B.   Labour Force Approach to Measure Disguised Underemployment—Work and Income Norm

IB (1).   Mujumdar's Method of Measuring Disguised Underemployment in Bombay, Karnatak Regions (india)

In his studies on the extent of disguised unemployment in some villages in Bombay, N. A. Mujumdar relies on a cultivator's desire and willingness for additional work, but he rejects the "time norm" as a measure of the phenomenon (156).   Explanation of disguised unemployment on "time norm" according to Mujumdar, are not suitable for analyzing the problem of agricultural work. Quoting L. E. Howard (89, p. 115) "in truth, the practical difficulties of applying anything that can be called an eight-hour day in agriculture are so obvious that it becomes doubtful whether it is worthwhile embarrassing public opinion with a discussion theoretically on the basis of the eight-hour day in agriculture." This is according to D. R. Gadgil (66 p. 15), "because the business of a family farm or of domestic industry does not require that punctuality in hours of work or regularity of attention and attendance which is required of a machine operator or attendant."

Thus, rejecting any "time norm," Mujumdar recommends a "work norm," i.e. a measure of quantity of work handled by a farm worker in a year and in this connection, he suggests a concept of "standard holding" as a criterion of full employment.   He defines a "standard holding" as the size of farm which, under the existing conditions of techniques, provides full employment for a family of average size, working with such assistance as is customary in agricultural operations (156, p. 83). In emphasizing the importance of the standard holding, he quotes George Obrein: "the size of farms largely affects the period of employment of labor and efficient use of farm equipment" and Thomas Edger, "the discussion on the acreage basis lends itself admirably to a discussion of the correlation between the size of the holding and its economic characteristics."

For determining the size of standard holding, Mujumdar divided the area into four homogeneous tracts and selected nine villages with 25 households from each village for investigation. A detailed questionnaire was drawn to elicit information on population, occupational classification of families, land utilization, areas under different crops, distribution of holdings, livestock, subsidiary occupations, etc. To determine the size of the "standard holding," households were asked the following questions:

(a) Do you think that the size of your holding is inadequate to give you enough employment and income?

(b) If more land was offered to you, are you able to cultivate it (with the existing pair of bullocks)? If yes, how many more acres can you cultivate?

As a check on the information furnished by landlords, village records were consulted to obtain information on the various characteristics of the holdings and discussions were held with experienced cultivators and knowledgeable village officials.

After establishing the size of the "standard holding" for each village, Mujumdar measured the intensity of employment of the households by comparing it with the size of holdings actually cultivated. The households were classified into:

(i) Standard cultivators who cultivate holdings of at least the size of the standard unit. They are fully employed cultivators.

(ii) Small cultivators who have holdings smaller than the standard unit. They are underemployed and the degree of their underemployment is indicated by the ratio between the "cultivated holding" and "standard holding."

(iii) Larger cultivators whose holdings are of a bigger size than a standard holding. They have families large enough to meet the labour requirements of big holdings and, as such, the norm of a standard holding does not apply to the larger cultivators.

After this classification, Mujumdar calculates the extent of disguised unemployment amongst the small cultivators as below:

(i) Percentage of farmers having less than normal employment, 71.4 per cent.
(ii) Percentage of farmers having less than half the normal employment, 52.7 per cent.

On the basis of these results, Mujumdar estimates the "surplus" or unutilized labour:

(a) Assuming that 52 per cent of cultivators have about one half of the normal employment, it can be said that 26 per cent of them are unutilized.
(b) If, further assuming, the remaining 19 per cent had three-fourths of the normal employment, it can be said that about 5 per cent of them are surplus. In this way, disguised unemployment was estimated at 31 per cent of the total farm workers.

Mujumdar found the response from the cultivators on their desire for additional land quite consistent and not exaggerated. He also found cultivators quite aware of their capacities to cultivate land. Mujumdar does not offer any solution to solve the problem of disguised unemployment. The study is intended only to show the superiority of the work over the "time norm" especially in farming programmes for fuller employment (156, p. 87). Some shortcomings in Mujumdar's methodology are mentioned below:

(i) He makes no attempt to quantify labour inputs. His results show only the proportion of underemployed cultivators, but the extent of their underemployment is not indicated. In the absence of this information, no policy can be formulated to utilize the surplus rural manpower in economic development process.

(ii) Mujumdar excluded (*a*) big cultivators (cultivating holdings larger in size than the standard holding), and (*b*) agricultural labourers. This exclusion would render the results to be grossly underestimated, especially in the areas where agricultural labourers form a considerable part of the total rural work-force. This measurement method is not applicable in rural economics like those in many parts of the Middle East with landlords owning the land and employing workers as tenants.

(iii) Mujumdar's assumption of employment, being a function of the size of the holding only, is rather an over-simplification. Irrigation, capital intensity, cropping system are two important determinants of rural employment and output to be ignored.

(iv) Mujumdar fails to relate his empirical results to his theoretical definition of disguised unemployment. He has defined the phenomenon as: "taking the size of labour force as given, disguised unemployment may be ascribed as a situation in which the withdrawal of a certain quantity of the factor labour to other uses will not diminish the total output of the sector from which it is withdrawn, *given* a measure of reorganization in the sector" (156, p. 39).

Due to these shortcomings, in our opinion, Mujumdar's method of estimating disguised unemployment has little operational value.

I. C. GAINFUL WORKER APPROACH

In this approach to the measurement of disguised unemployment, information on labour inputs employed on farm is obtained diretly from the households. But to estimate the amount of labour inputs required to maintain the existing output, various criteria are formulated, some of which are discussed below.

I. C. (1) PATTERN OF EMPLOYMENT OF AGRICULTURAL WAGE LABOURERS AS A DETERMINANT OF OPTIMUM LABOUR REQUIRED TO ESTIMATE DISGUISED UNEMPLOYMENT

For estimating the extent of disguised unemployment in South Korean agriculture in 1959, Yong Sam Cho (31) uses the employment pattern of agricultural wage labourers as a criterion to compute the amount of labour inputs required.

LABOUR INPUTS AVAILABLE AND EMPLOYED. Cho makes use of the farm data collected monthly by the research department of the Bank of Korea, the Korean Agricultural Bank, and the Ministry of Agriculture and Forestry of the Korean Government. Out of the 1,412 farm administrative districts with 2,256,161 farm households, a sample of 60 districts was selected. Those attending schools and engaged principally in household duties and other non-farming occupations were excluded from the total labour available, being designated as "not in the labour force." The farm workers (men, women and childern) were converted into homogeneous labour units by labour coefficients; 1.0 for the male farm workers of 15 to 59years of age, and 0.6 for the female farm workers in the same age-group. These labour coefficients were fixed according to the differential labour efficiency as reflected by the prevailing rural wage rates. The total farm workers were thus estimated and were converted into labour hours, at the rate of eight hours per day and 280 working days per year.

Extent and Classification of Unemployment. After computing the labour hours available and actually employed in Korean agriculture, Cho calculates the extent of underemployment for each month of the year. Cho's method of estimating underemployment is thus far similar to the land survey approach employed in the Indian National Sample Surveys and Puerto Rican labour surveys. Cho, however, goes further, and classifies underemployment into two categories: (*a*) seasonal unemployment (he refers to it as 'technical underemployment'), and (*b*) 'traditional disguised unemployment to discuss the removal of surplus labour off the farms. To explain traditional disguised unemployment, Cho describes a "socially marginal man"[1] who is free from tradition and custom. An attached agricultural worker[2] in the Korean agriculture conforms to Cho's "socially marginal man," since he

[1]Socially marginal men, according to Cho (31, p. 141) are those most susceptible to making new adjustments in situations of change, see also Chapter Three.

[2]An attached wage labourer, according to Cho, is one who is hired, not occasionally and intermittently like casual labourers, but regularly works in this capacity at least one-half of his total employment time.

is not employed in the traditional sense like a joint family farm worker and is "as fully employed as possible" (31, p. 6). When such social and cultural institutions as the joint family have disappeared from Korean society, family farm workers will be employed on the land like attached wage workers. With this assertion, Cho uses the employment pattern of attached wage labourers as a yardstick to estimate "tradition directed unemployment" that can be removed from agriculture for employment elsewhere, either under totalitarian methods or after the traditional institutions have changed. Seasonal underemployment (which Cho calls technical underemployment) is the truly removable surplus labour under *ceteris paribus* conditions. The "technical underemployment" is visible, while about the nature of tradition-directed underemployment Cho is not clear. He calls it a closed type of underemployment, and at the same time makes the statement:

...the underemployment we measured is all visible, not disguised in the sense of the traditional school.... Technical underemployment has nothing disguised or hidden about it. Where tradition directed underemployment is concerned, however, there is something there which draws a veil over it. It follows, therefore, that if the term 'disguised' has any meaning, it is this tradition directed employment which is, in a sense, disguised (31, p. 96).

The various classifications of underemployment used by Cho may be mentioned below.

Let TLE represent total labour inputs at present employed and TLA total labour inputs available, "Y" stands for rate of employment of the attached rural wage labourers.

TLA—TLE		= Total unemployment
$\dfrac{\text{TLE}}{r}$	=a	= Labour inputs required in the hypothetical tradition-free society
TLA—a		= Tradition-directed underemployment
a—TLE		= Technical underemployment

The estimates of underemployment arrived at by Cho for South Korean agriculture in 1959 are:

Total labour (family and wage) available TLA	$=2,358,221$ labour hours
Total labour (family and wage) employed TLE	$=1,640,942$ labour hours
Total underemployment	$= 717,279$ labour hours
Total underemployment as per cent of TLA	$= 30.42$ labour hours
Rate of employment of attached farm wage workers (r)	$= 0.8573$
Amount of labour required $\dfrac{(TLE)}{(r)}$	$=1,914,081$ labour hours
Technical underemployment $\left\{\dfrac{TLE}{r}-TLE\right\}$	$=273,139$ labour hours
Technical underemployment as per cent of TLA	$= 11.58$
Tradition-directed underemployment $TLA-\dfrac{TLE}{r}=$	$444,140$ labour hours
Tradition-directed underemployment as per cent of TLA	$= 18.83$

What are the policy implications of the above classification of underemployment? The present underemployment (TLA—TLE), according to Cho, can be utilized on the labour intensive labour projects in the villages. As regards tradition-directed and technical underemployment, the operational value of these concepts will be only in a hypothetical socially changed society. Cho seems to be aware of the elusiveness and vagueness of his notion of "social change" when he remarks, "a sudden breakdown of prevailing social institutions is an important conjecture in this study; the assumption is made, of course, for purely analytical purposes" (31, p. 96).

The main reasons for taking the employment pattern of attached wage labourers at a full employment level are: (*i*) that the attached wage labourer is "utilized as fully as possible," and (*ii*) that the attached wage labourer is not hindered by any tradition.

We have already discussed the question in Chapter two while

analysing relation between wage rate and zero marginal productivity. Our conclusion was that the wage rate of an agricultural labourer is related to his marginal product and also that his employment pattern could be, generally speaking, considered to constitute "full employment." Though we generally agree that attached agricultural labourers are comparatively free from tradition and customs inhibiting mobility, some non-economic factors still enter into their hiring practices and employment pattern as discussed in Section I. B. (2), Chapter two. In this connection, the remarks of the Second Agricultural Labour Inquiry Committee, 1956-57, (India) are very pertinent: "Left to themselves, agricultural labourers are rather immobile, bound as they are by conservatism, tradition and customs not to leave the place to which they belong and the cultivators with whom they are working" (95, p. 94).

I. C. (2) OUTPUT OF WELL-MANAGED FARMS AS A CRITERION TO DETERMINE OPTIMUM LABOUR REQUIRED TO ESTIMATE DISGUISED UNEMPLOYMENT.

At the instance of the Netherlands Ministry of Agriculture and Fisheries, the Agricultural Economics Research Institute (122) undertook a project to analyse economic aspects of underemployment in the Netherlands agriculture in September 1960. According to the Institute, "underemployment in farming can be taken to indicate that the density of labour in a given scheme and in given conditions of production is too high" (122, p. 4). The purpose of the project was to find out the present pattern of Dutch farm labour utilization and to determine the extent of underemployed labour that could be encouraged to quit farming to better their economic condition elsewhere. Through a sample survey, farm data relating to the size of farm, number of labour inputs available with number of days actually being employed and the physical quantity of agricultural produce (including livestock production) were collected for the year 1957, from the farm record kept by the Institute with cooperation from the farmers. To estimate the extent of underemployment, "standard hours", i.e. the number of labour-hours put in by a full labour unit to produce various agricultural crops, including livestock on the mixed farms of 10 to 15 h.a. during 1948, was taken as a norm. Using this norm, the standard units were calculated at 2,900. After computing the "labour effect" (actual full-labour units in use) and "standard full labour units" (i.e. full-labour units required), a comparison between them was made for various farm sizes. The extent of underemployment was equal to the difference between the "labour effect" and the "Standard Unit." The Institute has cited an example to illustrate the method. Take the farms on which, in 1957, 1,550 full-labour units were actually employed. At the fixed norm of 2,900 standard hours per full-labour unit, only 1,175 full-labour units should have been employed. So, in this case, the excess labour is 375 or the extent of disguised unemployment on these farms is about 25 per cent of the rural work-force. This estimate for all the farms, taken together, has been put at 11 per cent (122, p. 71). The Institute has remarked that this labour surplus can be removed only by increasing mechanization and rationalization.

What are the reasons for adopting 1948 labour productivity as a norm for measuring the extent of underemployment in 1957 ? This is because the Agricultural Economic Research Institute wanted to find the trend of labour productivity on the farms during the period 1949-1958. According to the Institute, despite the mechanization of agriculture and the exodus of farm workers from the land in the post-Second World War period, the density of labour on small farms (5 to 20 hectares) is extremely high. To reduce this high density of labour, steps have been taken to use land more intensively and to provide subsidiary work like raising cattle and poultry. To what extent these steps have been useful can be estimated, according to the Institute, by comparing the "labour effect" in 1957 with the "labour standard" of 1948 (122, p. 23).

The objective of measuring underemployment in the Netherlands was to judge the effectiveness of certain changes made in the farm resources. If the extent of disguised unemployment is to be estimated under *ceteris paribus* conditions, this method is not of much relevance to us. It raises an important question, however. Can we take some well-managed farms, such as a government experimental farm, or a privately managed farm recipient of an award for raising maximum output per acre[3] or a cooperative farm

[3]In India, the Government gives awards every year on the basis of maximum output per acre for certain crops.

and adopt their labour productivity as a norm to estimate the surplus manpower on other farms?

It is interesting to compare the characteristics of family and cooperative farms in Ludhiana District (Punjab, India), collected by H.S. Mann (136) in his study on experience with cooperative farming in Punjab. Mann took, for comparison, one cooperative farm and five individual family farm-holdings of varying sizes from 5.5 acres to 53 acres. Some comparative features are tabulated in Table 4.

It will be observed that the cooperative farms and the individual holdings are non-comparable in the matter of technique of cultivation. Explaining the farm equipment on the cooperative farm, Mann mentions: "The cooperative society used a Fordson Major tractor 28-32 h. p. which was purchased in August 1951 along with accessories. Two pumping sets 10 h. p. each and one h. p. engine for chaffcutting were also installed" (136, p. 106).

The cultivation on the individual holdings, on the other hand, is done by use of bullocks (note data on bullocks per 100 acres in able 4). Indian cooperative farms get various financial and technical facilities from the government which are not available to the individual farms. Due to the non-comparable features of the cooperative and individual farms, we tend to agree with Otto Schiller's remarks on this question. "It would be misleading to compare cooperative farms, to which State help is given in the form of advice, credit or. subsidies, with individual farms left without any help" (220, P. 5).

I. C (3) Subsistence Income Level as a Determinant of Optimum Labour Required to Estimate the Extent of Surplus Labour—A Production Function Approach

According to N. K. Sarkar (218), the employment problem in the agriculture of the underdeveloped countries is the high labour-supply relative to land and working capital. Due to the institution of joint family system, where the members share their work, chronic underemployment exists on the land. Defining surplus labour, Sarkar remarks, "surplus labour exists if the value of the marginal product of labour is less than the rate of the wage paid. The amount of surplus is to be measured by the excess of actual employment over

TABLE 4

EMPLOYMENT AND OUTPUT ON COOPERATIVE AND FAMILY FARMS

Characteristics	Cooperative Farm Size (acres)	Family Farm Holdings				
		A	B	C	D	E
Size of holding (acres)	.....	53	25	21	13.50	5.50
Workers per 100 acres held	5.46	5.66	10.0	9.52	13.89	23.50
Number of bullocks per 100 acres	2.70	7.60	16.0	9.50	16.70	23.50
Net income (Rs.) per acre for 1953	42.55	35.45	5.84	—14.24	99.10	—68.30

the employment which equates marginal productivity and the wage rate" (218, p. 209). But, since the mode of employment in peasant agriculture is not wage-payment, the members of a joint family share in the common family pool. Sarkar takes the marginal product of family farm labour and equates it with the family subsistence level. This is because, according to Sarkar, "when labour is increasing with the avenues of employment remaining limited and non-expanding or expanding at a slower rate, the marginal productivity is usually assumed to be tending towards the subsistence level" (218, p. 212).

To estimate the extent of surplus labour, Sarkar obtained information on the labour-days actually put in and estimated the optimum labour-units required. He collected statistics on the size and composition of labour used (in labour hours), size of holdings and non-labour money costs and output in bushels of rice in some districts in Ceylon, where the peasant problem was acute. Labour employed was standardized into units of "labour days" on the basis of eight hours work by males and sixteen hours by females.

For estimating the labour-days required, Sarkar fitted a Cobb-Douglas type of production function to the farm data and he obtained the following results:

$$Y = 1.988345 \ x_1 \ 0.0802 \ x_2 \ 0.5570 \ x_3 \ 0.2453$$

(x_1 is land in acres, x_2 days, x_3 non-labour costs in rupees and Y for output in bushels.)

He differentiates this equation with respect to labour to obtain the marginal product of labour (in bushels). This he equates with the subsistence level, which he arbitrarily takes as being the "standard of living indicated by per capita expenditure of the lowest income group at a particular point of time." In this way, Sarkar calculates the optimum labour-days (i.e. quantity of labour-days such that the value of the marginal physical product is equal to the subsistence level) required for each farm-size. Subtracting these optimum days from the actual labour-days employed, he computed surplus labour-days. In this way, Sarkar estimated the surplus labour-force at being 28.42 per cent of the labour-force.

I. C (4) ZERO MARGINAL PRODUCT AS CRITERION OF OPTIMUM
LABOUR REQUIRED TO ESTIMATE THE EXTENT OF DISGUISED UN-
EMPLOYMENT—A PRODUCTION FUNCTION APPROACH

John W. Mellor and Robert D. Stevens (140) undertook a study
of the marginal and average product of farm labour in Thailand
based on labour-income records, obtained by personal interview
from 104 representative rice farms located in the Central Plains, 20
miles north-east of Bangkok. These farms have uniform, flat, alluvial soil, identical capital investment and technique of cultivation.
The timing of production processes, the tools used and all aspects
of rice culture are traditional and standardized. In this way, Mellor
and Stevens assume that all farms have similar rice-production
functions. Labour inputs were measured in terms of "man equivalent" (a man equivalent equals 12 man-hours of available time for
farm work by an adult, aged 15 and above). Discussing the method
of estimating labour equivalents, Mellor and Stevens remark,
"Labor that is available for farm work but is doing no work is
counted as part of labor input. Labor that is actually used on the
fields but contributing no increment in output through its efforts
is not treated differently from labor that is not working but available for such work" (140, p. 785). Mellor and Stevens call this a
"stock of labor approach."

To estimate the productivity of labour, they fitted a least square
linear regression equation, given below:

$$Y = 30.4 + 13.5 \, X$$

(Y is the total product and X is the number of man equivalent.)

The b value (slope) in the equation is 13.5 tang which is equal to
approximately 0.54 bushels. This is not significantly different
from zero at five per cent level of significance. "This is consistent
with the hypothesis that in this type of an area, the marginal product of labor will be zero or close to zero" (140, p. 787).[4]   It is,
thus, an indication of the existence of disguised unemployment in
this area on the rice farms. Discussing the characteristics of this

[4]The value of the coefficient of correlation ($\overset{r}{xy}$) is not given. From the
scatter diagram, however, the value of *r* seems to be negligible. It implies very
little association between the labour and output.

unemployment, Mellor and Stevens remark:

> The presence of a large block of labor that apparently could be removed from agriculture with little effect on the volume of total agricultural production indicates the prime importance, as is generally recognized, of introducing new employment opportunities to areas of the type discussed (140, p. 789).

We will examine the measurement attempt with reference to (*a*) the validity of the method and (*b*) accuracy of the data used and the nature of the fit of regression line. As regards the technique, it is, in our opinion, a valid method of measuring the marginal productivity of labour. The labour inputs used beyond the level of zero marginal productivity are disguised unemployment as per their definition. The criterion used by Mellor and Stevens in estimating "labor equivalent" is open to questions. One can understand the exclusion from the labour force of children below 15 years, but why should there not be an upper-age limit as well ? The authors are aware of the limitations of the data and the inappropriateness of taking "labour stock" for labour inputs available on the farms, as Mellor recently admitted, "that data were inadequate for more than a rough approximation of disguised unemployment" (142, p. 2). It would be appropriate to quote below the comments on this study by Harry Oshima.

> There is one empirical study...of 104 farms in one Thai village. In this pioneer study, the conclusion is reached that there is substantial zero MPP farm workers. I feel it is hazardous to regard this study as conclusive for either theoretical or policy use (173, p. 450).

Commenting on the assumption of linear relation in the production function, Oshima remarks that:

> the spread of the data in the scatter diagram relating rice yields to labor inputs for each of the 104 farms suggests to me, not a linear regression line as it does to the author, but inadequate data and/or dubious assumptions (173, p. 450).

In our opinion, given the assumption of labour homogeneity, uniformity of capital investment and good fit of the regression line, the study is of definite theoretical interest since it suggests a satisfactory technique for testing the presence of disguised unemployment of labour with zero marginal product.

I.C. (5) ROSENSTEIN-RODAN'S STUDY IN SOUTHERN ITALY— A LABOUR DIAGRAM APPROACH

Asserting that, "it is our firm belief that disguised unemployment of more than 5 per cent exists in many, though not all underdeveloped countries," Rosenstein-Rodan (211, p. 1) made an attempt to measure disguised underemployment in Southern Italy in 1956. He gives the following definition of various types of disguised unemployment :

STATIC—Agricultural population that can be removed without any change in the method of cultivation, without leading to any reduction in the output. The marginal productivity of labour, in other words, is zero.

DYNAMIC SURPLUS—The agricultural population removed from agriculture without any reduction in total output on the assumption of a change in the method of cultivation. He distinguishes between the two sub-types of dynamic surplus depending on the nature of changes envisaged.

(*i*) Dynamic potential surplus: on the assumption of a small change in method of cultivation permitting only re-arrangement of work with but small additions of circulating capital.

(*ii*) True dynamic surplus: on the assumption of thorough changes including additional use of the both fixed and variable captial.

Rosenstein-Rodan attempted to measure disguised unemployment, only in a static sense, calling it a "basic concept having a clear and unequivocal meaning." He applied a direct method of measurement, collecting information about "labour available" and "labour required" from a sample of 100 farm holdings through questionnaires and distinguishing between different types of cultivation, sizes and forms of property and the composition of labour force, etc. The following major assumptions were used:

(*i*) Only small agricultural holdings of direct cultivators (peasant-owners and tenants) were included. Agricultural labourers were excluded on the ground that these would not be surplus, though he admits the possibility of their partial underemployment.

(*ii*) The active population was assumed to be between fourteen and sixty-five years of age. Coefficients of labour efficiency of men, women, and children were used for each type of cultivation.

(*iii*) Surplus workers were assumed to be involuntarily unemployed.

(*iv*) Labour hours required for each type of cultivation over the whole year, month by month, were counted and compared with available labour hours. An average of 270 available work-days per year was assumed.

(*v*) A distinction was made between (*a*) disguised true removable unemployment—entire labour units who are unemployed throughout the year and whose removal would not lower agricultural output; (*b*) disguised fractional unemployment —labour hours not used throughout the whole year and that do not add up to an entire labour unit, and thus, cannot be removed outside agriculture; (*c*) Seasonal underemployment due to climatic factors. These distinctions were taken into account in calculating the number of labourers affected by disguised unemployment.

(*vi*) A slight deviation from the static concept was allowed, in that hiring additional labour for a peak load up to 50 working days during a year was assumed to be a tolerable minimal change compatible with static assumption of *ceteris paribus*.

Rosenstein-Rodan found that "more than 10 per cent of the active labor force in Southern Italian agriculture is surplus" (211, p. 4).

This study evokes several comments. First, he has ignored the social and cultural barriers hindering the removal of surplus farm workers from joint families and village environments. Secondly, complete exclusion of hired agricultural labourers would underestimate the results if the family farm workers are also working as hired labourers on part-time basis.

II. INDIRECT METHODS OF MEASUREMENT OF DISGUISED UNEMPLOYMENT

In indirect method of measuring disguised unemployment, information on the "labour inputs" available and "required" is obtained from secondary sources. We shall now examine some indirect methods used in different countries.

II. A. TIME-WORKED APPROACH

II. A. (I) MEASUREMENT OF SURPLUS LABOUR IN GREEK AGRICULTURE

The Center of Economic Research in Athens has published a macro-study conducted by Adam A. Pepelasis and Pan A. Yotopoulos (186) to estimate the surplus labour in Greece.

(*a*) *Removable Chronic Surplus Labour* was defined as:

> taking techniques, crop-mix and the quantities of the other factors of production at their historically given levels (with the exception of a routine reorganization of the work force), we estimate the amount of agricultural labor which could have been removed from farms for at least a complete year without any reduction in output (186, p. 30).

Since this chronic surplus labour is removable for at least a complete year, it is, in fact, the "difference between the peak season actual employment and full employment levels" (186, p. 24).

(*b*) *Seasonal Surplus labour*, "contributes to the productive operation for a part of year only and can be withdrawn accordingly from the fields only intermittently" (186, p. 28).

(*c*) *Labour Available*. The size of agricultural population for 1953-60 was derived from the census of 1951 and supplemented by a pilot census in 1960. Persons between the ages 15 to 69 years were considered as the "working age population" from which the labor potential" was estimated by excluding "labor not available," like disabled persons and those confined in prisons or mental institutions, in retirement, attending schools, etc. The potential agricultural labour was converted into homogeneous units, "man productive units" (MPU) on the basis of a conversion coefficient; (boys—ages: 15-19 and adult women: 20-64 = 0.70 MPU; girls between 15 and 19 years = 0.60 MPU*)*. These conversion coefficients were adopted on the basis of wage rates for men, women, and children. Multiplying those man-productive units by the potential number of working days per year for agricultural activities (arrived at 255 work-days per year after taking into account Sundays, national and religious holidays, climatic factors, agricultural work done inside home, etc.), man-productive days (MPD's) were computed for the years 1953-60, and this constituted "labour available" in the Greek agriculture.

(*d*) *Labour Required*—Separate estimates of the annual labour requirements for farming (all crops, including vegetables, fruits, and cattle feed), animal husbandry, forestry, fishing, and agricultural transport were computed. Taking figures on cultivated areas devoted to different agricultural products and other agricultural activities in animal husbandry, forestry, and fishing from government statistical reports, annual labour requirements by products and other agricultural activities were estimated by applying "labour intensity coefficient" (labour/land or labour/capital ratios). These labour intensity coefficients (originally computed by Evelpides (61) on the basis of a sample survey of several farms in different agricultural activities in different areas of Greece, where experts observed the amount of time which the farmers actually spent in performing each agricultural operation) were supplemented by the authors with labour requirements for fishing and agricultural transport. These labour-coefficients were revised for different years by taking into account changes in methods of cultivation, including mechanization in seeds and crop varieties and in institutional agricultural set-up like land consolidation.

By comparing these estimates of "labour available" and "labour required," the authors computed figures about "chronic labour surplus" and "seasonal surplus labour." Explaining their results, Pepelasis and Yotopoulos remark, "Chronic surplus labor in Greek agriculture is virtually non-existent. From the eight years of our series it existed only in 1953 and 1954 to the extent of 3.5 per cent and 2.3 per cent respectively. The other years of the period are marked by a seasonal shortage of labor" (186, p. 136). About the seasonal surplus labour, the authors remark, "winter is consistently the season of highest surplus (ranging from 24 to 31 per cent of the labour force in different years) and the fall presents the lowest degree of seasonal surplus labour—from 5.1 per cent and 4.0 per cent for 1953 and 1954, and 1.2 per cent to 6.0 per cent in other years between 1955 and 1960." Discussing the policy implications of these findings, they recommend "supplementing off-season work-load by creating part-time work in handicrafts, local public works, and community development."

Though we shall discuss the general usefulness of the indirect approach in measuring disguised unemployment at the end of this section, a contradiction between their definition of surplus labour and on the results of the study may be pointed out. Defining the concept of chronic surplus labour, the authors originally remarked that, "such chronically unemployed labor may be considered as contributing nothing to the productive activities and, therefore, as directly removable" (186, p. 29). In explaining their conclusions, they commented on the feasibility of removing the chronically unemployed by noting, "if in one village of 100 working agricultural population, the surplus labor is 2 per cent, this does not imply that we can remove for a whole year two workers without decreasing the total output of the village" (186, p. 138).

II. A (2) AN ESTIMATE OF RURAL UNEMPLOYMENT IN ALIGARH (UTTAR PRADESH, INDIA) AND IDAGARI (MADRAS, INDIA)

S.S. Gupta (75) undertook a project to estimate the extent of under-employment in twenty-four villages in the Aligarh District, Uttar Pradesh (India) during June 1950, by comparing agricultural man-hours available and man-hours required each day. For estimating man-hours available, Gupta obtained information from a survey of the villages on the number of men, women, and children of land-owners and landless families in the age-group of 11 to 60 years. For estimating man-hours required per day, labour time needed for raising different crops and for performing other agricultural operations (this can be called labour/output ratio or labour coefficient) was determined on the basis of Indian crop calendar, September 1950, issued by the Economic and Statistical Adviser, Ministry of Food and Agriculture, Government of India, and publications like *Agricultural Wages in India*, Volume I, issued by the Ministry of Labour, and from his personal observation.[5] Using these labour coefficients, area under crops and intensity of work in

---

[5]Gupta does not furnish details of estimating man-hours required for raising different crops and for performing other agricultural operations.

various agricultural operations, Gupta estimated total number of man-hours required at 1,759.71 per day against 22,688 man-hours available. From these figures, Gupta concluded that the disguised unemployment problem in the villages surveyed by him was severe. Gupta commented:

It can be easily conceded that the above method is not hundred per cent accurate but it gives a fairly accurate idea of the problem. In the absence of a better alternative, this method can be a good guide and our planners should give it a trial (75, p. 386).

Gupta's method of estimating underemployment has many unexplained gaps. On what basis did he formulate "efficiency ratios" for converting men, women, and children into standard labour units? His estimating labour-hours required and labour-hours available on per day basis is unsatisfactory. The results obtained on a one-day basis are too dependent on chance factors to be reliable in policy formulation.

Along the same lines, M. Srinivasan (241) estimated rural under-employment in Idagari—a village in Coimbatore District, South India (1951). From the Census Report, combined with a survey of the village, Srinivasan estimated adult rural population and converted it into man-days. According to the Economic Adviser to Madras Government, the labour force has capacity and willing-ness to work 260 days a year (241, p. 177). For estimating the man-days required, Srinivasan took labour coefficients (i.e. labour/land ratio which gives the number of labour-days required in different agricultural operations for raising each crop per acre of land) from the information bulletin issued by the Madras Department of Agriculture.[6] Multiplying this ratio to the acreage under various crops (obtained from the revenue records of the village), Srinivasan calculated estimates of total man-days required. The difference between the man-days available (154, p. 440) and man-days required (115, p. 475) gave 38,965 man-days (about 33.7 per cent of the available labour force) which constituted disguised unemployment in this village. Discussing the value of these results, Srinivasan remarks, "such a technique can only furnish rough but service-able estimates. Actual figures are laborious to compute"...(241,

[6]Srinivasan has not furnished details on estimating the time required to raise crops, which was used as a criterion to measure disguised unemployment.

p. 178). Furthermore,

> rural unemployment will provide a clue to the waste of labour resources in agriculture and the extent of industrialization necessary to divert this waste to productive and beneficial activities...the technical training, vocational education and simple mechanical implements necessary to set up cottage industries to engage this labour can be gauged from figures of rural unemployment (241, p. 175).

II. A. (3) An Evaluation of the Indirect Method of Measuring Disguised Unemployment with Time-Worked Approach

This indirect method of estimating disguised rural unemployment, through using the norm of "labour time required to cultivate a unit of land, or to produce a unit of output" is crude and rough. As remarked by Rosenstein-Rodan, "...the results are highly imprecise, since the amount of labour required cannot be exactly established" (211, p. 5). In farming, the various tasks are so numerous and varied that it is difficult to obtain accurate estimates of labour required. Due to the influence of climatic factors on agricultural operations in underdeveloped economies where agriculture is a gamble with nature, the "labour time required" norm would differ every year.

Furthermore, using the census figures to estimate "agricultural manpower available" is beset with many difficulties. Usually, to estimate "available manpower," all persons of appropriate ages classified as "agriculturists" in census reports are assumed to be available for farm work. Actually, in rural areas an exact enumeration of different occupations and identifying them with different age-groups of individuals are complicated tasks in the underdeveloped countries. As pointed out by P. K. Mukerji, "an individual has to carry on more than one or two occupations to get just a subsistence living" (158, p. 57). Classifying two or more occupations of a family into the main and secondary occupations may create problems, since, as remarked by Mukerji again,

> data about occupations are generally collected from informants by interview method and direct questions are put to them about

their occupations. In case of households with more than one occupation, the judgment as to which of their occupations is principal and which of them is secondary is generally left to their discretion (158, p. 57).

In view of these enumeration problems in census data, any estimates on "agricultural manpower available" based on it should be interpreted with great caution in regard to their dependability for basing conclusions for policy recommendations.

This method is, however, simple to apply and entails comparatively little effort and time to estimate the extent of disguised unemployment. In the circumstances, where a high degree of accuracy is not desired and the objective is merely to have a general idea about the existence of disguised unemployment, this method could well be used.

II. B. WORK AND INCOME APPROACH

In this approach, the norm for "labour required" is formulated in terms of units of work (land or income) deemed necessary to provide a worker and his family with full employment. A comparison of this norm with actual number of work units put in indicates the extent of disguised unemployment. In most studies of this nature, the land area deemed necessary to provide the average family with: (*a*) full employment, or (*b*) a decent standard of living is adopted as a work norm. The terms "standard holding," "optimum holding" and "economic holding" have been used in this connection. The main arguments in support of the "work and income approach" as against the "time worked" approach have already been noted in this chapter while examining the work of N. A. Mujumdar in Bombay and Karnatak.

II. B. (1) MEASUREMENT OF UNDEREMPLOYMENT IN POLAND

The European Conference on Rural Life in 1939 suggested that on an assumption of mixed husbandry and importance of cereal crops, about 12.4 acres might be taken as a family unit for a family of five with two workers. This would mean about 2.5 acres per head and 6.2 acres per worker. Comparing the size of family unit with the actual sizes of the holdings in Poland, 80 to 90 per cent of the holdings in the sub-Carpathian lowlands of Poland were found below this size. According to the European Conference on Rural Life, the position in other East European countries was scarcely better. On this basis, the existence of severe underemployment was indicated in Poland in 1939.

II. B. (2) MEASUREMENT OF DISGUISED UNEMPLOYMENT IN INDIA

M. L. Gupta (74) used the concept of "economic holding" in estimating the extent of disguised unemployment in Indian agriculture for the year 1953. Gupta was aware of the fact that the size of economic holding was a matter of personal approximation. After taking into account factors like climate, nature of crops, technique of cultivation, etc. Gupta made a conservative estimate on the size of "economic holdings" for different qualities of land as below:

Quality of Land	Size of Economic Holding
Lands of high fertility	5.0 acres
Lands of medium fertility	7.5 acres
Lands of low fertility	10.0 acres

According to Gupta, farms of the above sizes, "would provide opportunities for the full-time use of the available labour of families cultivating lands of the different qualities" (74). Assuming that the quality of land is indicated by the degree of its population density, and also that, during the course of more than 2,000 years of Indian

TABLE 5

TOTAL ACREAGE REQUIRED CALCULATED ON THE BASIS OF ESTIMATED SIZE OF ECONOMIC HOLDING

Geographical regions according to population density	Regional population (millions)	Rural males employed in agriculture (millions)	Size of economic holding (acres)	Total acreage required (million acres)
High density	184.5	29.92	5.0	144.60
Medium density	97.4	15.23	7.5	114.23
Low density	79.2	12.40	10.0	1240.0
Total	361.1	56.55		382.83

history, her population has been distributed in different regions according to the variations in the land's fertility, Gupta divided India in three regions according to population density on the basis of figures from Indian Census of 1951. He took the population of each region and the number of rural males employed (assuming rural males as heads of families), and calculated total acreage required on the basis of estimated size of economic holdings as shown in Table 5.

Against this 382.83 million acres, required to provide full employment to farm families in 1951 (raised to 386.83 million acres in 1953, taking into account population growth during the years 1951-53), the total area sown during that year was 270 million acres, thus estimating a shortage of 117 million acres. Assuming 7.5 acres as the size of economic holding for all grades of land in India, this shortage of land indicates disguised unemployment of about 15.6 million rural male heads of households in India in 1953.

II. B (3)   AN EVALUATION OF THE INDIRECT METHOD OF MEASURING DISGUISED UNEMPLOYMENT WITH WORK AND INCOME APPROACH

The concept "economic holding" (also synonymous with terms, "basic holding," "optimum holding," "family holding," "standard holding" and "full employment holding") is one of those elusive and vague terms that are not easily amenable to precise definition. Economic holding has varying interpretations. Keatinge defines it as one "which allows a man a chance of producing sufficient to support himself and his family in reasonable comfort after paying his necessary expenses." H. S. Mann defines economic holding as the size of farm "which will provide for an average family minimum standard of life considered satisfactory," while Stanley Jevons interprets it as one "which will provide a high standard of life for the farmer." Another definition is, "which will give the most profitable employment at the highest possible net returns to the capital and labour which an average cultivator's family can command" (111, p. 59). Terms like "reasonable," "minimum" and "decent" used for standard of living are vague and indeterminate and involve humanistic and ethical value judgments. The vagueness in the interpretations of the term is evident from the proposed size for an economic holding. For a Deccan village in Western India, H. S. Mann suggested 20 acres as a size of "economic holding," and Keatinge suggested a size of 40-50 acres. As a matter of fact, the concept of "optimum holding" or "economic holding" is dependent on so many variables as, for example, the average size of a family, quality of land, productivity of labour, degree of mechanization, income, value of crops, and existence of subsidiary earnings, that the results will differ not only from country to country, but also from region to region and from farm to farm. Gupta (74) is quite correct in his remarks that the size of economic holding is a matter of personal guess and approximation, and in the circumstances its use as a norm to estimate the extent of disguised unemployment would lead to very crude and undependable results.

III-A CONCLUSION

In this chapter, we examined different methods that have been used to estimate the extent of disguised unemployment in agriculture in various countries. In our evaluation of these methods, we tried to observe the weakness and strength of these methods with special reference to their suitability in measuring the extent of the pheno-menon in the rural sector of an underdeveloped economy like India. We classified various methods of measurement under two categories: (*i*) direct method, and (*ii*) indirect method, depending on the sources of data. In the direct method, we distinguish between the "labour force" and "gainful worker" approaches. In the former approach, the worker's judgment on his level of work activity is accepted as a basis for determining his intensity of employment, while in the latter approach, distinction is drawn between the labour time being actually put in by a worker and the labour time required, determined on the basis of some "norm." We found the "gainful worker" approach more appropriate to measure the extent of dis-guised unemployment. We then examined "time worked" versus "work and income" approaches and our preference was in favour of the former because of the ambiguity and vagueness involved in terms like "economic holding" with reference to which "work unit" is usually measured. In the indirect method, we similarly examined techniques using "time worked" and "work and income criteria." Our main conclusion about the "indirect method" was that, while it is simple and inexpensive in terms of both time and effort, the results obtained therefrom are usually too crude to be useful for policy recommendations. After examining various techniques, the "direct method" using "gainful worker" criterion with "time worked" approach seems more suitable to determine the extent of disguised unemployment in rural sector of an underdeveloped country. The data required for such a method of measuring disguised unemployment is outlined below.

III. B   DATA REQUIRED TO MEASURE DISGUISED UNEMPLOYMENT

(a) A sample of households to be studied should be carefully selected with reference to its representativeness of the area. In selecting the sample, the area should be divided into units homogeneous in climate including rainfall, soil conditions, technique of cultivation, communications and marketing system, etc.

(b) Data for labour inputs employed:
(*i*) occupation and age distribution of members of each household. Non-working population (children, the old, voluntarily unemployed, etc.)is to be excluded from the labour force;
(*ii*) the number of man-days put in by each working member including agricultural labourers (both casual and permanent) in various agricultural operations for each holding during different months of the year. The agricultural work should include time put in crop production, tending of cattle, and marketing of produce but should exclude the labour put in non-agricultural operations like trade and business, cottage and small-scale industries. This information should be collected separately for irrigated and non-irrigated parts;
(*iii*) the agricultural wages prevalent in the area required for converting the labour inputs of women and children into homogeneous labour units—man-days equivalents; and
(*iv*) the size of the holdings, in respect of each household along with information on items like proportion of total area irrigated, fragmentation of holdings, intensity of cropping, and cropping pattern.

(c) Data required for determining the labour inputs required—Information on the following main factors affecting agricultural output and employment is needed.

(*i*) Investment on each holding during the year under study on various items like fertilizers, types and value of agricultural implements and their maintenance; employment of bullock labour and their maintenance cost;

(*ii*) value of agricultural output (crops—food and commercial crops, dairy products), marketed or self-consumed for each holding; and

(*iii*) labour inputs required for "maintenance activities," e.g. keeping irrigation ditches free of weeds, digging ditches for preventing soil erosion and waterlogging, repair of the cattle sheds and other farm buildings, etc.

The use of above information in measuring the extent of disguised unemployment is illustrated in the next chapter.

CHAPTER FIVE

MEASUREMENT OF DISGUISED UNEMPLOYMENT IN PUNJAB AGRICULTURE

In this chapter, an effort will be made to estimate the extent of disguised unemployment in the agriculture of Punjab (India), by applying a simple "direct method gainful worker approach."[1] To estimate the extent of this category of disguised unemployment, we have to find a difference between the number of labour-days being put in various agricultural operations and the number of labour-days actually required on the farms for the existing total agricultural output. The data required to estimate the labour-days "actually employed" and "really required" have been specified in the previous chapter. We are, however, aware of the fact that in many underdeveloped countries such elaborate data are not available; and we must temporarily be contented with rough estimates. In connection with plans for economic development, some underdeveloped countries are becoming increasingly aware of the need for collecting adequate and reliable data on various socio-economic aspects of the national life. In India, public and private research organizations have undertaken to collect data on various sectors of the economy.

National Sample Surveys have been in operation since 1945 and have collected valuable statistics on the diverse social and economic topics on all-India basis. Recognizing the importance of farm management data as a help in drawing up programmes for development of agriculture in India, the Planning Commission initiated the Studies in Economics of Farm Management for six

[1] I am greatly indebted to Professor Hans J. A. Kreyberg, Visiting Professor of Economics, University of Minnesota, from Institute for Socialokonomi Norges Tekniske, Trondheim, Norway, for his valuable suggestions in applying this method.

The method is mentioned in the writings of Viner (263, p. 19), and Leibenstein (125).

major agricultural regions in India (including Punjab) for the year 1954-55, to collect from a sample of villages representing all the agricultural regions, statistics on physical features, soils, rainfall, revenue division, population, communication and marketing system, land utilization and irrigation systems, cropped area and intensity of cropping, pattern of cropping, production and livestock, both through the cost accounting and survey sample methods. These studies are continued on a yearly basis and the latest statistics available on the Punjab Agriculture pertain to the year 1956-57 (99). For the Punjab study, 200 holdings were selected for the cost accounting analysis[2] from the two contiguous districts of Amritsar and Ferozepore, representing the typical soil, climate and crop complex of the state of Punjab.

Commenting on the representative character of the data the report for the year 1956-57 states:

It is thus clear that (i) the villages selected in the sample are quite representative of the two districts and (ii) that holdings selected represent the agricultural economic conditions in the selected villages fairly well (99, p. 196).

A serious limitation of the Farm Management Studies report may be noted. The figures relating to the level of employment, output, investment, etc. per acre have been given in tables, against different holding sizes, classified in five groups, (*i*) 0 to 5 acres, (*ii*) 5 to 10 acres, (*iii*) 10 to 20 acres, (*iv*) 20 to 50 acres, (*v*) 50 acres and above. It is a pity that the valuable and comprehensive data collected in these surveys have been published in such a scant form, giving us as few as five observations in many cells. This constitutes a serious drawback in the matter of analysing the data. Since we could find no other more detailed Indian data, we have decided to use this grouped data as given in the Report for the year 1956-57 for estimating the extent of disguised unemployment.

Like the rest of Indian rural society, the farm households of Punjab are set up on the basis of the joint (or extended) family system with an average size of 8.1 members.

---

[2]In the cost accounting, complete farm accounts for the whole year on sample farms are maintained by the investigator in collaboration with the farmers.

A perusal of Table 6 will indicate that, except in the largest farms (50 acres and over), the bulk of farm labour is provided by family members. The proportion of farm labour, put in by hired workers, increases while that of the family workers decreases with increase in the size of the holding. Because of the high proportion of hired farm labourers on holdings of above 50 acres, these are not regarded as family farms.

We shall now estimate the extent of disguised unemployment. We shall refer to labour input required as a "standard quantity of labour" which can be defined as the minimum number of labour input required to produce the existing output with other factors remaining the same. In order to find the "standard quantity of labour," we would observe the farm output per acre on holdings of different sizes on the assumption that 'other factors' affecting the employment and output are alike on the different holding sizes. If we find that on the bigger holdings (with smaller labour input) the farm output per acre is equal to that on the smaller holdings, we would be able to estimate the relation between output and labour input per acre that would give us the required "standard labour input." But, before we proceed to examine the farm data to locate such a standard point, we should see to what extent "other factors" are alike on different sizes of holdings. Wherever we observe variations in these factors, we shall attempt to bring the data to a uniform level by minimizing the effects of these differences.

Numerous factors determine the level of farm output and employment, some of which, along with their main impact on employment and output, have been listed in Tables 7 and 8. In many respects, conditions on farms of different sizes are identical. The climatic factors of weather and rainfall over the region are all fairly uniform, and the textural composition of soil of alluvial origin and the terrain of the plain are also identical over the entire region. From the data in Table 8, it would appear that the quality of land and soil (indicated by approximately equal value of land per acre) is the same. The quantity of fertilizers used per acre by the bigger landholders is not larger than that used by the smaller cultivators. The figures relating to cropping pattern (Table 8, columns 2 and 3) show that among the four smaller size-groups, the percentage of area devoted to food crops and commercial crops does not vary a great deal.

On the largest size-group (50 acres or more), however, commercial crops are grown on a much greater proportion of the total area cropped than food crops. In this respect, farms in this size-group are not typical of the region. The technique of cultivation, as evident from the figures relating to the employment of bullock labour per acre cropped, the value of investment on implements and machinery per acre held, and the value of capital investment (except the value of land) per acre does not show significant variation between the farm sizes.

The factors in which we find great variation in different size-groups are the intensity of cropping (percentage of total area sown) and the percentage of area irrigated. These greatly influence the level of employment and agricultural output per acre, as indicated in the columns 6 and 9 in Table 7. The man-days per cropped irrigated acre are about double the number of man-days on the cropped unirrigated acres. Similarly, the value of gross output per unirrigated acre held is about half that of the gross output per irrigated acre held. In order to minimize the difference in these two factors, it is proposed to take the gross output and employment per acre on the cropped irrigated area for estimating the standard quality of labour. Since our focus in this study is on employment, we would use the ratio of labour input per acre cropped on irrigated and unirrigated areas for converting the unirrigated area into irrigated area equivalent in each size-group.[3] These calculations have been made and the total area cropped in irrigated acres is shown in Table 9.

I. COMPUTATION

Now we can estimate the 'standard' amount of labour input per acre. We shall have to compute gross output and labour input employed per cropped irrigated acre on the farms of different sizes. These computations are given in Table 10. For farms of 0-5 acres, with 41.61 man-days per acre, we get gross output of Rs. 151.67 per acre. As we move to larger farms, we find that smaller labour input produces gross output per acre, generally equal to or greater

---

[3]Unirrigated acres have been converted into irrigated area equivalent by the formula.

$$Z = X.Y$$

Where X = Unirrigated cropped area [acres]

Y = Ratio of labour inputs [man-days] on unirrigated and irrigated cropped area.

Z = Irrigated area equivalent.

TABLE 6

NUMBER OF PERMANENT FARM WORKERS, (PERMANENT FARM LABOURERS AND FAMILY WORKERS) IN PUNJAB AGRICULTURE

Holding size groups (acres)	Number of holdings	Total area held (acres)	Average size of holding (acres)	Total number of permanent farm workers engaged (man units)			Percentage of total farm workers	
				Family	Hired	Total	Family workers	Farm Labourers
(1)	(2)	(3)	(4)	(5)	(6)	(7)	(8)	(9)
0 to 5	15	54.54	3.63	17.00	—	17.00	100.0	—
5 to 10	48	359.44	7.48	73.00	3.25	76.25	95.7	4.3
10 to 20	76	1091.85	14.36	145.67	13.48	159.15	91.5	8.5
20 to 50	57	6671.33	29.32	135.75	38.17	173.92	78.0	22.0
50 or more	4	318.99	79.74	3.67	6.10	9.77	37.6	62.4
Total or average	200	3496.15	17.48	375.09	61.00	436.09	86.0	14.0

Notes : (i) Permanent farm workers include family and farm labourers hired on definite contracts for a regular period that may range from 2 to 3 months in a year. To convert farm workers of different age-groups into homogeneous man-units, an adult who worked on the farm all the year has been taken as one worker, while one who spent only three months, as equivalent to 0.25 worker, and with six months' service as half a worker, a male worker above 16 years of age has been taken as one worker while a woman and a child have each been considered equal to 0.75 and 0.50 worker respectively. (ii) Besides these permanent farm workers (family workers and permanent farm labourers), some casual workers are employed for a few days for specific jobs to cope with the rush of work in peak seasons. The number of days per acre held during which casual labour is employed do not vary significantly on different holding sizes; they are 2.77, 2.17, 1.05 and 2·69 man-days for size-groups of 5 to 10, 10 to 20, 20 to 50 and 50 or more respectively. The results in columns (8) and (9) above are unaffected.

Source : Government of India, Ministry of Food and Agriculture, *Studies in Economics of Farm Management in Punjab, Report for the year 1956-57*, 1962, pp. 8, 9, 40, 209.

TABLE 7

LANDHOLDINGS IN AMRITSAR AND FEROZEPORE DISTRICTS, 1956-57

Holding size -groups (acres)	Per cent irri- gated to total area held	Intensity of cropping*			Labour input per cropped acre (man-days = **)		Gross output per acre held (Rs.)	
		Irrigated	Unirrigated	Total	Irrigated	Unirrigated	Irrigated	Unirrigated
(1)	(2)	(3)	(4)	(5)	(6)	(7)	(8)	(9)
0— 5	89.20	177.64	123.46	171.80	24.2	12.8	265.10	135.27
5—10	85.50	154.14	123.56	149.70	23.7	14.1	224.89	113.37
10—20	74.87	147.19	106.80	137.04	21.7	12.6	225.73	98.30
20—50	65.88	135.18	105.74	125.14	22.3	11.3	223.64	106.61
50 or more	87.15	119.69	100.00	117.16	16.1	7.1	161.91	45.58

Source: Directorate of Economics, and Statistics, Government of India, *Studies in Economics of Farm Management in Punjab*, 1956-57, pp. 12, 60, 84, 86, 209.

*Intensity of cropping=total area shown as per cent of total area held.

**Man-day=8 hours of work.

TABLE 8

LANDHOLDINGS IN AMRITSAR AND FEROZEPORE DISTRICTS, 1956—57

Holding size-groups (acres)	Cropping pattern (percent of cropped irrigated acre under)		Average value of land per acre (Rs.)	Employment of bullock labour per acre cropped (days)	Investment on implements and machinery per acre held (Rs.)	Value of fertilizers used per acre held (Rs.)	Investment on farms (excluding value of land per acre held) (Rs.)
	Food crops	Commercial crops					
(1)	(2)	(3)	(4)	(5)	(6)	(7)	(8)
0— 5	59.3	14.3	664.54	15.6	8.50	0.89	422.99
5—10	57.9	12.9	507.31	16.7	5.52	0.54	286.55
10—20	56.3	17.5	534.12	15.5	5.00	0.34	267.86
20—50	52.6	20.0	618.18	14.20	5.29	0.29	184.97
50 or more	25.1	45.6	521.52	11,7	5.51	0.80	183.61

Source: Directorate of Economics and Statistics, Government of India, *Studies in Economics of Farm Management in Punjab*, Report for the year 1956-57, pp. 17, 21, 22, 29, 30, 33, 59, 62, 79, 88 and 89.

TABLE 9

ACREAGE OF IRRIGATED AREA EQUIVALENT

| Holding size-groups (acres) | Total area held (acres) | Total area cropped* | | | Ratio of labour input on un-irrigated and irrigated cropped area (per acre) | Unirrigated crop-ped area conver-ted into cropped irrigated area equivalent (acres) | Total irrigated area equivalent (acres) |
		Irrigated	Unirrigated	Total			
(1)	(2)	(3)	(4)	(5)	(6)	(7)	(8)
0— 5	54.54	86.44	7.26	93.70	12.8/24.2	3.85	90.39
5—10	359.44	473.65	64.45	558.70	14.1/23.7	38.28	511.93
10—20	1,091.85	1,203.26	293.05	1,496.31	12.6/21.7	169.97	1,373.25
20—50	1,671.33	1,488.45	603.06	2,091.51	11.3/22.3	301.53	1,789.98
50 or more	318.99	332.74	41.00	373.74	7.1/16.1	18.04	350.78
All Groups	3,496.15	3,584.54	1,008.82	4,593.36		531.67	4,116.21

Source: Directorate of Economics and Statistics, Government of India, *Studies in Economics of Farm Management in Punjab*, 1956-57, pp. 84, 85, 209.

*Multiplying the total irrigated and unirrigated area held by their respective intensities of cropping (columns 3 and 4 in Table 7), we get total area cropped in columns 3 and 4 above. Since an acre of land is cultivated more than once during a year, the area cropped would exceed the area held.

TABLE 10

LABOUR INPUT AND GROSS OUTPUT PER ACRE (IRRIGATED AREA EQUIVALENT), PUNJAB, 1956-57

Holding size-group (acres)	Total area irrigated equivalent (acres)	Total labour input* employed on all holdings (man-days)	Labour input** (man-days) per irrigated acre	Total gross output on holding Rs.	Gross output per irrigated equivalent acre in rupees
(1)	(2)	(3)	(4)	(5)	(6)
0—5	90.29	3,757	41.61	13,694.99	151.67
5—10	511.93	20,007	39.10	75,004.34	146.51
10—20	1,373.23	46,836	34.10	211,513.18	154.02
20—50	1,789.98	54,437	30.41	307,023.32	171.52
50 and above	350.78	5,878	16.75	46,878.77	133.64

*To calculate the total man-days employed on all holdings in different size-groups, we have multiplied the number of permanent farm workers (family workers and permanent servants) from column 7 in Table 6 by the figures on average annual employment of a permanent farm worker given in Farm Management Report 1956-57 (p. 39), also including the labour input of casual labourers.

**Labour input per irrigated equivalent acre has been calculated by dividing total labour input employed on all holdings (col. 3) by total irrigated equivalent area (column 2—computed in columns 6 and 7 in Table 9). These figures are quite different from labour input per irrigated and unirrigated cropped acres (columns 6 and 7 in Table 7). The latter represent labour input employed separately on irrigated and unirrigated cropped acres, while the figures in column 4 above are labour inputs per acre if all the unirrigated acres were converted into irrigated equivalent by the ratio of labour inputs now employed on irrigated and unirrigated land.

Source: Directorate of Economics and Statistics, Government of India, *Studies in Economics of Farm Management in Punjab*, 1956-57, p. 39, 84.

than those on smaller farms (except for a minor deviation on size of 5-10 acres). On 20-50 acre farms, with 30.41 man-days (compared to 41.61, 39.10 and 34.10 man-days on smaller ones), we have gross output of the value of Rs. 171.5 per acre (against Rs. 151.67, Rs. 146.51, and Rs. 154.02 on smaller size-groups). The labour input decreases further on the farms larger than 50 acres, but in our opinion, these are not family farms at all, and they differ from the other farms in the following respects:

(*i*) The pattern of cropping (the proportion of the area devoted to food and commercial crops) on these farms is different from the others. See columns 2 and 3 in Table 8.

(*ii*) We can see from column 8 in Table 6 that the number of family workers, as a proportion of the total farm work-force, is very low—only 37.6 per cent against 78 to 100 per cent on other size-groups.

These seem to be commercial farms (indicated by cropping pattern), cultivated mainly by hired labour, as against the family farms in the other size-groups. This statement is supported further with reference to the ceiling on agricultural holdings per family, fixed in the land reform legislation, enacted in different states of India. In Punjab, the ceiling fixed is 30 standard[4] acres, or ordinary 60 acres; in the case of displaced persons from Pakistan, it is 40 standard acres or 100 ordinary acres (93, p. 231). Tea plantations, orchards, specialized farms engaged in cattle-breeding, commercial crops and cooperative farms are exempt from the ceiling. The farm of 50 acres and more in the sample seems to belong to this exempt category and, thus, their output and employment cannot be used as "standard labour input." In the circumstances, our choice falls on the 20 to 50 acre size-group to determine the amount of labour required to maintain the existing total agricultural output under existing conditions. We note from Table 10 that on holdings of the size of 20 to 50 acres, with 30.41 man-days, the gross output per acre is Rs. 171.52. As already noted, most of the 'other factors' determining the farm output and employment do not vary significantly on the holdings of different sizes, and further, we have adjusted for

---

[4]A standard acre means an acre of land yielding between 10 and 11 maunds of wheat (93, p. 237). One maund=82 pounds.

the differences based on 'cropping intensity' and 'irrigation' factors. We can, thus, assert that if the small holdings below the size of 20 acres are consolidated, the employment output relationship on them would be similar to that on 20 to 50 acres size-group. On this basis, we have taken 30.41 man-days as the "standard labour input" per acre and, assuming consolidation of holdings, labour employed over and above the standard labour input is tantamount to disguised unemployment. Observing the labour input employed and output per irrigated equivalent acre on different holding sizes, we find more labour input on all size-groups below 20 acres than the standard labour input. We, thus conclude that disguised unemployment of labour exists to an extent estimated (Table 6) at 8.41 per cent of the total labour-force. On the smaller size holdings, the magnitude of the phenomenon is quite high. For instance, on the farms of less than 10 acres, more than one–fifth of the labour-force seems excessive.

Our method of measuring the extent of disguised unemployment is free from many shortcomings, usually found in other measurement attempts (29, 147, 186, 210). The labour-force working on the farms is based on the actual number of persons employed along with the number of days at work, rather than on estimates from the census reports, etc. Our estimates of labour units required on the farms are free from the arbitrary norms of "work norm" or "time norm." These are not based on vague and elusive standard like "optimum" or "economic holdings," "optimum density of population," etc. but have been derived from careful analysis of relationship between the level of employment and output on various holding sizes.

We are, however, aware of the limitations of our estimates. Some have arisen because the data were tabulated by only five sub-groups so that we have only five ratios to compare. The breakdown of the data into more sub-groups would have been very helpful in providing us with more accurate results.

Further limitations in our measurement technique are pointed out below:

(i) The criterion of "standard labour input" (30.41 man-days per irrigated equivalent acre as on the 20-50 acre farms) indicates the level of employment free from disguised unemployment. If, however, the actual labour input for the "standard labour

TABLE 11

DISGUISED UNEMPLOYMENT OF FARM WORKERS IN PUNJAB, 1956-57

Holding size-groups (acres)	Total no. of man-days employed	Total no. of man-days required (estimated)	Disguised unemployment in man-days	Disguised unemployment as % of total labour-force
(1)	(2)	(3)	(4)=(2)—(3)	(5)
0— 5	3,757	2,746	1,011	26.90
5—10	20,007	15,568	4,439	22.18
10—20	46,836	41,760	5,076	10.83
20—50	54,437	54,437	—	
All groups	125,037	114,511	10,526	8.41

input" is lower than 30.41 man-days or in other words, if 30.41 labour input contains some disguised unemployment, our results of 8.41 per cent disguised unemployment would be an underestimate. If our data were broken into more sub-groups, we could prepare more accurate estimate of standard labour input.

(*ii*) We noted from columns 6 and 7 in Table 7, that the man-days per cropped irrigated acre are about double the number of man-days per cropped unirrigated acre. In order to remove this difference, we converted the unirrigated area into an irrigated area equivalent, on the basis of the ratio of their labour input (Table 9). This assumes that the proportion of disguised unemployment is the same on irrigated and unirrigated lands. If the magnitude of disguised unemployment is lower on the irrigated land because of many small leisure-time jobs to be done, like deepening the drains and maintenance of irrigation equipment, our converting unirrigated acres to an equivalent of irrigated acres, would lower our estimates of disguised unemployment. Because of these limitations, these estimates of disguised unemployment are rough and by no means conclusive.

II. COMPARISON OF OUR RESULTS WITH OTHER STUDIES:

Our estimate of 8 per cent disguised unemployment for Punjab agriculture is below the figure of 25-35 per cent assumed by the Indian Planning Commission for such unemployment in the Second Five Year Plan (93, p. 315) for the Indian rural economy as a whole. This comparatively low level of disguised unemployment in Punjab is supported by the following observations on the employment pattern in the state:

(*i*) The Board of Economic Inquiry, Punjab (194) conducted a survey of the rural unemployment in Punjab in 1955. From information on the intensity of employment (number of months per year worked) collected from the household directly through interview method, the Board estimated that while 42 per cent of the workers were underemployed (working less than 9 months in a year), only 10 per cent of them were severely underemployed (working less than 6 months in a year).

(*ii*) Analysing the utilization of manpower in Punjab, the National Council of Applied Economic Research, New Delhi has remarked:

In the rural areas, unemployment mostly appears in the form of underemployment. As a result of the more intensive techniques of cultivation employed and larger area cultivated by the average farmer, it is likely that he puts in a larger number of man-hours of work than his counterpart elsewhere in the country. All this may amount to this that underemployment, and consequently unemployment, may not be such a serious problem in rural Punjab as a whole as elsewhere in India (161 p. 52).

According to the report of the Second Agricultural Labour Enquiry Committee, 1956-57 (95, pp. 70-1), cultivators in Punjab are employed for larger number of days per year than their counterparts in other states in India. The Agricultural Labour Enquiry Committee has furnished the following figures on the employment pattern of agricultural labourers in different states of India:

TABLE 12

EMPLOYMENT PATTERN OF AGRICULTURAL LABOURERS IN DIFFERENT STATES OF INDIA

State	Total number of days employed per year	State	Total number of days employed per year
Uttar Pradesh	221.79	Madras	192.90
Madhya Pradesh	210.75	Kerala	170.19
Bihar	220.36	Bombay	240.94
West Bengal	241.52	Mysore	217.14
Orissa	206.43	Rajasthan	214.76
Andhra Pradesh	229.41	Punjab	244.18

(*iii*) In studying the impact of the Second World War on Indian economic conditions, A. R. Prest (190) mentions the existence of surplus labour in Indian agriculture. According to Prest, despite the witdrawal of 5 million persons from agriculture for war efforts, the area of cultivated land output per acre and the cropping pattern remained more or less constant during the years 1939-45. In regard to Punjab, however, according to Prest, "where recruiting was strong, the supply of agricultural labour was far from plentiful" (190, p. 30).

CHAPTER SIX
CONCLUSIONS

IN THIS study we attempted to review the literature on the subject of disguised unemployment—its nature and measurement. Confusion exists in the literature because the same terminology has been applied to explain different, and often inconsistent, situations. There is controversy regarding the existence and importance of disguised unemployment because writers, who question one particular type of disguised unemployment, frequently challenge the entire concept, without considering alternative interpretations. Conclusions, based on the measurement of one particular type of disguised unemployment, have been generalized as if they were valid for the phenomenon in general.

The study was divided into two parts. The first part was devoted to a survey of the theory of disguised unemployment. With a view to organizing the literature in logically consistent categories, the following theoretical framework distinguishing the main causes of disguised unemployment was formulated:

(1) Disguised unemployment due to a deficiency of aggregated demand.
(2) Disguised unemployment due to structural causes.
   (a) Imperfections in particular labour markets:
   (i) Immobility of labour both geographical and between alternative occupations.
   (ii) Errors in planning vocational training.
   (b) Disguised unemployment due to an excess aggregate labour-supply relative to the aggregate supplies of cooperating inputs.

The literature was surveyed under the above classifications with special reference to the social and economic conditions in the rural sectors of the underdeveloped countries. It was found that disguised unemployment due to a deficiency of aggregate demand is not of primary importance in such economies. As regards disguised unemployment arising from imperfections in particular labour markets, the situation is certainly not peculiar to under-developed economies, though it may be more pronounced than in advanced economies.

The primary cause of disguised unemployment in many agrarian societies is believed to be the excess aggregate labour-supply rela-tive to the aggregate supplies of cooperating factors. Theoretical models illustrating the emergence of disguised unemployment from this inappropriate factor endowment under different forms of organization of the firm, viz. family firm, commercial firm operated by a profit maximizing entrepreneur with hired workers, etc. were formulated, and the phenomenon of disguised unemployment was classified under the following categories:

(1) The marginal physical product of labour is zero in the strict static sense. Labour can be withdrawn from a family enterprise without any reduction in total output and without introducing any change either in the quantity or quality of the cooperating inputs.

(2) The marginal physical product is actually positive in the strict static sense and the removal of labour from family farms would reduce total output, but this fall in output would be small and could be offset by a modest increase in the quantity of coope-rating inputs or a modest improvement in the quality of the labour input.

(3) The marginal physical product is positive in the strict static sense; the removal of labour input would reduce the total output substantially and this fall could not be offset by modest changes in the quality or quantity of cooperating inputs.

The literature on each category of disguised unemployment was surveyed and the nature and logical foundation of the phenomenon were examined. The relevance and importance of these categories to the social and economic conditions in the rural sector of an underdeveloped economy were also discussed. As regards the con-troversial question whether the marginal product of a disguised unemployed labour could fall to zero or not, our conclusion, after examining both the arguments and the results of empirical studies, was that it was a matter of empirical research, and certainly, the empirical issue could not be decided on the basis of *a priori* reasoning and casual observation. There is nothing in the production theory which denies the possibility that a sufficiently large increase in one input can reduce its marginal product to zero.

Then followed a description of the theoretical models relating disguised unemployment to the stages of development by which a dual economy—with a family-firm sector and hired-labour sector—is gradually converted into an exclusively hired-labour economy. In connection with the removal of surplus manpower from the farms for utilization in the economic development process, the role of the social and cultural institutions of an underdeveloped economy was emphasized.

Part II of the study is concerned with the measurement of disguised unemployment. We classified the techniques employed in various parts of the world under the following headings.

I. *Direct Methods of Measurement:* Involving empirical enquiries using questionnaires designed to ascertain directly from households information on the extent of labour utilization, i.e. labour-time, actually worked as a proportion of total labour-time households were willing and able to supply.

II. *Indirect Methods of Measurement:* In these methods of measuring disguised unemployment, information relating to labour input, available and required, was obtained from such secondary sources as census reports and occupational surveys, etc.

(a) TIME-WORKED NORM: Using man-hours as the unit of labour input.

(b) WORK AND INCOME NORM: Using the amount of work done (e.g. amount of land cultivated or output produced) as measure of labour input.

(c) LABOUR-FORCE APPROACH: Workers' level of employment is determined on the basis of their willingness and ability to undertake additional work. The households are interviewed to obtain information on the amount of labour (in units of time or work) they are putting in, as compared with the amount of labour they would be able and willing to supply.

(d) GAINFUL WORKER APPROACH: In this case, information on labour input, actually put in on the farms is obtained directly from the households. But to estimate the amount of labour input required to maintain the existing level of output, various criteria are formulated including (1) employment pattern of the agricultural wage labourers, (2) labour input required on the well-managed farms, and (3) production function method of fitting regression lines.

We examined these measurement techniques with a view to formulating a suitable method to estimate the extent of disguised unemployment in the rural sector of an underdeveloped economy. After a critical evaluation of various techniques, we concluded that the "direct method of measurement" using a "time worked norm" is more appropriate for obtaining dependable estimates on disguised unemployment. The nature of the farm data required for this measurement technique was also specified. We then applied a method to estimate the extent of disguised unemployment in the agricultural sector in Punjab (India).

In Chapter Five, we analysed farm data collected by the government of India in connection with the farm management studies in the Punjab, relating to the year 1956-57. The data furnishes details of input and output for 200 farm holdings by a cost accounting method, and for 400 holdings by a sample survey method. Comparing the output and labour input per acre on various size-groups of farms, we estimated 30.41 man-days as the "standard labour input" required per acre for the existing output with present technique of cultivation and capital investment. On the basis of the standard labour input, we found that while the proportion of disguised unemployment is quite high on small size holdings (i.e. it is 26.90 and 22.18 per cent of the total labour force on the holding size-groups of 0-5 and 5-10 acres respectively), the over-all figure for all size-groups is 8.41 per cent. In the strict static sense, the marginal product of these disguised unemployed labour inputs is positive and small, but with consolidation of holdings, these labour inputs could be removed from the farms without reducing the total output.

BIBLIOGRAPHY

1. ADACHI, *Analysis of Over Population in Farming Community in Japan. A case of Ehime*, Matsuyama, 1955

2. AGGARWAL, P. N., "Unemployment in Villages," *Rural India*, 1954, Vol. XVII, pp. 18-20

3. AHMAD, C. G., "Extent and Utilization of Manpower Resources in Pakistan," *Economics and Commerce*, 1964, Vol. III, pp. 7-10

4. ARMENTROUT, W. W., "Employment and Underemployment in Rural People in the Appalachian Area," *Journal of Farm Economics*, 1959, Vol. XXXXI, pp. 1076-83

5. BAHADUR, P., "The Concept of Disguised Unemployment Reconsidered," *Indian Journal of Labour Economics*, 1960, Vol. III, pp. 76-86

6. BANSIL, P. C., "The Magnitude of Rural Unemployment," *Rural India* 1955, Vol. XVIII, pp. 225-30

7. BARBER, WILLIAM J., "Disguised Unemployment in Underdeveloped Economy," *Oxford Economic Papers*, February 1961, Vol. XIII, pp. 103-15

8. BAUER, PETER T., and YAMY BASIL S., *The Economics of Underdeveloped Countries*, New York, 1957

9. BELSHAW, H., "Economic Development of Asia," *Economia Internazionale*, 1952, Vol. IV, pp. 844-71

10. BERDECIA, F. S. and JAFFE, A. J., "The Concept of Measurement of Underemployment," *International Monthly Labor Review*, 1955, Vol. LXXVIII, pp. 283-7

11. BEVERIDGE, W., *Unemployment—A Problem of Industry*, London, 1931

12. BHAGWATI, J., "Unemployment Relative Prices and the Saving Potential," *Indian Economic Review*, 1958, Vol. IV, pp. 71-82

13. BHATIA, R. J., "Disguised Unemployment and Saving Potential," *Indian Economic Review*, 1958, Vol. IV, pp. 33-8

14. BHATT, V. V., "Underemployment in Underdeveloped Economies," *Indian Economic Journal*. July 1957, Vol. V, pp. 38-46

15. ―――――――――"Employment and Capital Formation in Underdeveloped Countries," *Economia Internazionale*, 1958, Vol. XI, pp. 121-36

16. BHATTACHARYYA, D., "Rural Underemployment—The Search for a Concept," *Economic Weekly*, 1957, Vol. IX, pp. 117-18

17. BICANIC, RUDOLF, "Three Concepts of Agricultural Overpopulation," in Roger N. Dixey (ed.), *International Exploration of Agricultural Economics*, 1964

18. BISHOP, C. E., "The Rural Development Program and Underdevelopment in Agriculture," *Journal of Farm Economics*, 1960, Vol. XXXXII, pp. 1196-1209

19. ————————, "Underemployment of Labor in South-Eastern Agriculture," *Journal of Farm Economics*, May 1954, Vol. XXXVI, pp. 258-72

20. BLEEKER, R. J. P. VAN GLINSTRA and MADEN F. H. VAN DER, "Emigration from the Netherlands, *International Labour Review*, May 1953, Vol. LXVII

21. BOEKE, J. H. *The Structure of Netherlands Indian Economy*, New York, 1942

22. BOOTOMLEY, ANTHONY, "On Road Building and the Economics of Underdeveloped Countries," *Economic Journal*, March 1964, Vol. LXXIV, pp. 231-3

23. BRONFENBRENNER, M. "Production Function : Cobb-Douglas, Interfirm Intrafirm," *Econometrica*, 1944, Vol. XII, pp. 35-44

24. ————————and DOUGLAS, P. H., "Cross Section Studies in the Cobb-Douglas Function," *Journal of Political Economy*, 1939, Vol. XXXXVII, pp. 761-85

25. ————————"Some Labor Economics of Dualism," *Paper read at the 1963 meetings of the American Association for Asian Studies at Philadelphia*

26. BUCK, JOHN LOSSING, *Chinese Farm Economy*, Chicago, 1930

27. ————————, *Land Utilization in China*, Chicago, 1937

28. CHANDAVARKAR, A. G., "The Saving Potential of Disguised Unemployment," *Economic Journal*, 1957, Vol. LXVII, pp. 335-8

29. CHIANG, HSIEH, "Underemployment in Asia: Nature and Extent," *International Labor Review*, January-June 1952, Vol. LV, pp. 703-25

30. ————————"Underemployment in Asia: Its Relation to Investment Policy," *International Labor Review*, July-December 1952, Vol. LVI, pp. 30-9

31. CHO, YOUNG SAM, *Disguised Unemployment in Underdeveloped Areas with Special Reference to South Korean Agriculture*, Berkeley, 1963

32. CLARK, COLIN, "Future Sources of Food Supply: Economic Problems," in *Food Supply and Population Growth*, London, 1963.

33. ————————, *Conditions of Economic Progress*, London, 1940

34. ————————and JONES, J. O., "The Production Functions for Average and Marginal Productivity of Land and Labor in English Agriculture," *Indian Journal of Agricultural Economics*, 1955, Vol. XI, pp. 117-53

35. COBB, C. W. and DOUGLAS P. A., "A Theory of Production," *American Economic Review*, 1928, Vol. XVIII, pp. 139-65

36. COOPER CHARLES A., *Agriculture Labor Surplus and Foreign Trade in Bulgaria 1925-60*, Unpublished doctoral dissertation

37. DALTON, GEORGE, "Traditional Production in Primitive African Econo-

mies," *Quarterly Journal of Economics*, August 1962, Vol. LXXVI, pp. 360-78

38. DANDEKAR, V. M., "Utilization of Rural Manpower," *Economic Weekly*, Annual Number 1962, pp. 267-76

39. ————————, *Use of Food Surplus for Economic Development*, Gokhale Institute of Politics and Economics Publications, Vol. XXXIII, 1956

40. ————————, "Economic Theory and Agrarian Reform," *Oxford Economic Papers*, February 1962, Vol. XIV, pp. 69-80

41. DANTWALA, M. L., "Notes on Some Aspects of Rural Employment," *Indian Journal of Economics*, 1953, Vol. VIII, pp. 19-32

42. DASS, N., *Unemployment, Full Employment and India*, Bombay, 1948

43. DAS GUPTA, A. K., "On the Assumption of Unlimited Supply of Labor," *Economic Weekly*, 1958, Vol. X, pp. 157-9

44. DAS GUPTA, S., "Underemployment: Its Conceptual and Statistical Issues," *Economic Weekly*, 1957, Vol. IX, pp. 1106-8

45. DATTA, BHABATOSH, *The Economics of Industrialization*, Calcutta, 1960.

46. DAVIS, KINGSLEY, *The Population of India and Pakistan*, New Jersey, 1951

47. DESHPANDE, S. H., "Labor Surpluses and Saving Potential in Under-developed Countries," *Indian Economic Journal*, January 1959, Vol. III, pp. 376-89

48. DEWETT, K. K., *Indian Economics*, Delhi, 1960

49. DEY, S. K., *Spare Time Production for Gain*, Food and Agricultural Organisation, Rome, 1960

50. DOUGLAS, P. H., *The Theory of Wages*, New York, 1934

51. ————————"Are There Laws of Production?" *American Economic Review*, 1948, Vol. XXXVIII, pp. 1-41

52. DOVRING, F., *Labor Used for Agricultural Production—An Attempt at a Fresh Approach to Productivity in Agriculture*, Urbana, 1963

53. ————————, *Land and Labor in Europe, 1900-1950*, The Hague, 1956.

54. DRIVER, P. N., "Measurement of Rural Unemployment," *Indian Journal of Agricultural Economics*, March 1954, Vol. IX, pp. 161-9

55. DUCOFF, LOUIS J. and HAGOOD, MARGARET J., "The Meaning and Measurement of Partial and Disguised Unemployment," *Population Studies*, 1953, Vol. XVII, pp. 249-50

56. DUESENBERRY, JAMES S., "Some Aspects of the Theory of Economic Development," *Exploration in Enterprise History*, December 1950, Vol. III, pp. 63-102

57. ECKAUS, R. S., "The Factor-Productions Problem in Underdeveloped Areas," *American Economic Review*, September 1955, reprinted in Aggarwal and Singh, ed. *The Economics of Underdevelopment*, New York, 1958.

58. EICHER, CARL and WITT LAWRENCE W., *Agriculture in Economic Development*, New York, 1964

59. EL-GHONEMEY, M. R., *Underemployment of Farm Labor in Egypt, A Report to the International Labour Organization*, Cairo, 1955

60. ENKE, S., "Economic Development with Unlimited and Limited Supplies of Labour," *Oxford Economic Papers*, New Series, June 1964, Vol. XIV, pp. 158-72

61. EVELPIDES., "Espiskopesis tes Agrotikes Economics tes' Hellados," *Agrotika Economia*, January—March 1957, Vol. XVI, pp. 21-45

62. EZEKIEL, HANNAN, "An Application of Leibenstein's Theory of Underemployment," *Journal of Political Economy*, October 1960, Vol. LXVIII, pp. 511-17

63. FRANKEL, HERBERT S., "United Nations Premier for Development," "*Quarterly Journal of Economics*, August 1952, Vol. LXVI, pp. 301-26

64. FRIEDMANN, E. A. and HAVIGHURST, Work and Retirement in Nosow and Forum, ed., *Man, Work and Society*, New York, 1962

65. FUKUOKA, MASO, "Full Employment and Constant Coefficients of Production," *Quarterly Journal of Economics*, February 1955, Vol. LIX, pp. 23-41

66. GADGIL, D. R., "Preconditions of Economic Development," *Indian Journal of Economics*, February 1952, Vol. I, pp. 14-20

67. GEORGESEU-ROEGEN, N., "Economic Theory and Agrarian Economics, *Oxford Economic Papers*, New Series, February 1960, Vol. XII, pp. 1-40

68. GHOSE, D., *Pressure of Population and Economic Efficiency in India*, New Delhi, 1946

69. GHOSE, S. K., "Underdevelopment in India," *Modern Review*, 1953, Vol. LXLIV, pp. 486-7

70. GILL, K. S., Keynesian Economics and Underdeveloped Countries," *Indian Economic Journal*, October 1954, Vol. II, pp. 119-30

71. GLEASON, ALLEN, H., "Chronic Underemployment"—A Comparison Between Japan and U.S.A., *The Annals of the Hitotsubashi Academy*, August 1959, Vol. I, pp. 64-80

72. GUDIN, EUGENIO, "Marginal Comments on the Problems of Underdeveloped Countries," *Wirstshafts Dienst*, May 1954

73. GUHA, S., "Unemployment and Underemployment," *Indian Economic Review*: 1958, Vol. X, pp. 11-16

74. GUPTA, M. L. *Problems of Unemployment in India*, 1955

75. GUPTA, SHANTI SWARUP, *A Study of Agricultural labour in the District of Aligarh* Unpublished doctoral dissertation, Aligarh University (India), 1959

76. HABERLER, GOTTFRIED, "Critical Observations on Some Current Notions in the Theory of Economic Development," L'Industria, 1957, Vol. II reprinted in George W. Beltz and N.K. Chaudhry, ed. *Readings in Economic Development*, 1963

77. HABIBULLAH, M., "Technique of Measuring Underemployment in Agriculture," *Dacca University Studies*, 1959, Vol. IX, pp. 93-9

78. HAIDER, S. M., "A Study of Population Pressure in Relation to Agricul-

tural Development in Pakistan," *Indian Economic Journal*, 1958, Vol. XXXVIII, pp. 239-48

79. HASAN, P., "Non-Inflationary Mobilization of Surplus Labor," *Selected Papers on Pakistan Economy*, 1958, Vol. III, pp. 94-106

80. HATHAWAY, DALE, E., *Government and Agriculture*, New York, 1963

81. HEADY, E. O., "Production Functions from a Random Sample of Farms," *Journal of Farm Economics*, 1960, Vol. LXX., pp. 114-24

82. —————————, *Agricultural Policy under Economic Development*, Ames, 1962

83. HENDRIX, W. E., "Income Improvement Prospects in Low Income and Underemployment," *Journal of Farm Economics* 1959, Vol. XXXXI, pp. 1065-75

84. HIGGINS, B., The Theory of Increasing Underemployment," *Economic Journal*, June, 1950, Vol. LX. pp. 255-74

85. HIGGINS, H. D., "Seasonal Variations and Employment in Jamaica," *Social and Economic Studies*, 1953, Vol. I, pp. 85-115.

86. HUGHES, R. B., "Demonstration Effect on Production," *Journal of Farm Economics*, August 1960, Vol. XXXXII, pp. 659-63

87. HITCH, THOMAS, "Meaning and Measurement of Full and Maximum Unemployment," *The Review of Economics and Statistics*, February 1951, Vol. XXXIII, pp. 1-11

88. HOREWOOD, J., "Overpopulation and Underemployment in the West Indies," *International Labour Review*, 1960, Vol. LXXXII, pp. 103-37

89. HOWARD, L. E., *Labour in Agriculture*, London, 1935

90. HUBBARD, LEONARD E., *The Economics of Soviet Agriculture*, London, 1939

91. HUSSAIN, MOHD., "Problem of Agricultural Labor in Pakistan," *Economic Digest*, 1958, Vol. I, pp. 367-72

92. HUZURTA ZAR, V. S., "A Note on the Survey of Employment, Income and Expenditure of the People in Sarvodaya Area in Ratnagiri District," *Bombay Economic and Statistical Bulletin*, 1951, Vol. V, pp. 13-35

93. INDIA, PLANNING COMMISSION, *Second Five Year Plan*, New Delhi, 1955

94. —————————, *Third Five Year Plan*, New Delhi, 1960

95. INDIA, MINISTRY OF LABOUR AND EMPLOYMENT, Agricultural Labour in India, *Report of the Second Enquiry Committee*, Vol. I, All India, New Delhi, 1960

96. INDIA, CABINET SECRETARIAT, *The National Sample Survey 9th Round Supplementary to Report No. 16*, May-November 1955, Vol. LXII, 1962

97. —————————, *Rural Work Programme*, New Delhi, 1964

98. INDIA, MINISTRY OF LABOUR, *Rural Man-Power and Occupational Structure*, New Delhi, 1964

99. INDIA, MINISTRY OF FOOD AND AGRICULTURE, Studies in the Economics of Farm Management in Punjab, *Report on the year 1956-57*, New Delhi, 1960

100. INTERNATIONAL BANK OF RECONSTRUCTION AND DEVELOPMENT, *Report on Cuba*, 1950

101. ISLAM, N., "Concepts and Measurements of Unemployment and Under-employment in Developing Economies," *International Labour Review*, March 1964, Vol. LXXXIX, 1964

102. INTERNATIONAL LABOUR OFFICE, *Action Against Unemployment*, Studies and Reports, New Series, No. 20, Geneva, 1950

103. ———— *Unemployment and Labour Force Statistics, A Study of Methods*, Studies and Reports, No. 7, Geneva, 1948

104. INTERNATIONAL LABOUR OFFICE, ASIAN ADVISORY COMMITTEE, *Underemployment in Asia, Its Causes and Remedies with Special Reference to Social Aspects of Capital Formation for Economic Development*, Geneva, 1951

105. ———— "Employment and Unemployment Statistics," *International Labour Review*, 1954

106. IYENGAR, S. K., "India's Unemployment Problem," *Capital*, Calcutta, 1955, pp. 43-5

107. ———— "Industrialization and Agriculture in India," *Economic Journal*, 1944, Vol. LIV, pp. 189-205

108. JAFFE, A. J. and STEWARD, C. D., *Manpower Resources and Utilization*, New York, 1951

109. JAKHADE, V. M., "Effects of Technical Change on Employment in Agriculture in India," *Reserve Bank of India Bulletin*, 1955, pp. 1191-7

110. JAPAN, BUREAU of STATISTICS, OFFICE of the PRIME MINISTER, *Report on the Special Survey of the Labor Force*, October 1955, March 1956, October 1956, March 1957, and October 1957

111. JATHER, G. B. and BERI, S. G., *Indian Economics*, Vol. I, Bombay, 1949

112. KAHLON, A. S., and BHARDWAJ, M.L., "Some Indicators of Farm Human Labour Productivity," *Indian Journal of Agricultural Economics* 1959, Vol. XIV, pp. 40-4

113. KALDOR, D. R. and BOUDER, W. W., *What Effects on Farms when Operators Take Jobs in Town*, Iowa Farm Society, December 1963, pp. 275-8

114. KALECKI, M., "Unemployment in Underdeveloped Countries," *Indian Journal of Labour Economics*, 1960, Vol. III, pp. 59-62

115. KENADJIAN, BERDJ, *Disguised Unemployment in Underdeveloped Countries*, Unpublished doctoral dissertation, Harvard University, 1957

116. KHAN, A. A., "Problems of Rural Labour and Wages in the West Punjab," *Pakistan Economic Journal*, 1949, Vol. I, pp. 40-61

117. KILBY, P., "African Labor Productivity Reconsidered," *Economic Journal*, June 1961, Vol. LXI, pp. 273-91

118. KOSTNER, N., "Some Comments on Professor Nurkse's Capital Accumulation in underdeveloped Countries," *L'Egypte Contemporaine*, April 1953, Vol. LXIV, pp. 1-8

119. KREEF, J. M., "Population Pressure and Economic Development in Indonesia," *American Journal of Economics and Sociology*, 1953, Vol. XII, pp. 355-71

120. KUMAR, D., "The Transfer of Surplus Labour From the Rural Sector," *Indian Economic Journal*, 1957, Vol. V, pp. 355-70

121. LAL, RAM NARESH, "Disguised Unemployment in Indian Agriculture and Its Saving Potential, *Indian Economic Journal*, July 1962, Vol. CLXVIII pp. 41-5

122. LAND-BOUW-ECONOMISCHS INSTITUTE, *Economic Aspects of Underemployment in Agriculture in the Netherlands*, January 1961.

123. LEBERGOTT, ST., "Measuring Unemployment," *Review of Economics and Statistics*, November 1954, Vol. XXXVI, pp. 390-450

124. LEE, HOON K., *Land Utilization and Rural Economy in Korea*, Chicago, 1936

125. LEIBENSTEIN, HARVEY, *Economic Backwardness and Economic Growth*, Science Ed., New York, 1963

126. —————, "The Theory of Underemployment in Backward Economies," *Journal of Political Economy*, 1959, Vol. LXV, pp. 91-103

127. —————, "Underemployment in Backward Economies, Some Additional Notes," *Journal of Political Economy*, 1958, Vol. LX, pp. 256-8

128. —————, "Reply to Oshima's Underemployment in Backward Economies," *Journal of Political Economy*, 1958, Vol. LXVI, p. 264

129. LEWIS, W. A., *The Theory of Economic Growth*, 1955

130. —————, "Economic Development with Unlimited Supplies of Labor," Manchester School, May 1954, reprinted in Aggrawala and Singh, ed. *The Economics of Underdevelopment*, New York 1958

131. —————, "Employment Policy in an Underdeveloped Area," *Social and Economic Studies*, September 1958, Vol. VII, pp. 42-54

132. McLOUGHLIN, PETER F. M., "The Need for a 'Full Employment' and Not a Disguised Unemployment Assumption in African Developing Theorizing," *Zeitschrift Fur Nationalokonomie*, Vol. XXII, pp. 362-8

133. MALTHUS, T. R., *An Essay on the Principle of Population*, London, 1798

134. MAMORIA, C., "Rural Unemployment," *Rural India*, 1952, Vol. XV, pp. 133-43

135. MANDELBAUM, K., *The Industrialization of Backward Areas*, Oxford, 1945

136. MANN, H. S., "The Experience of Co-operative Farming in Punjab," *Indian Journal of Agricultural Economics*, January—March 1958, Vol. XIII, pp. 100-8

137. MARUTA, S., 1956-1958 Memorandum, Faculty of Agriculture, Kagoshima University, in Colin Clark, *Food Supplies and Population Growth*, 1963

138. MAZUMDAR, D., "The Marginal Productivity Theory of Wages and Disguised Unemployment," *Review of Economic Studies*, 1956, Vol. XXVI, pp. 190-7

139. —————, "Underemployment in Agriculture and the Industrial Wage Rate," *Economica*, 1959, Vol. XXVI, pp. 328-40

140. MELLOR, JOHN W., and STEVENS, ROBERT D., "The Average and Marginal Product of Farm Labor in Underdeveloped, Economies *"Journal of Farm Economics,* August 1956, Vol. XXXVIII, pp. 780-91

141. ——————, and MOORTI, T.V., *Farm Business Analysis of 30 Farms in Midhekur, Agra, India, 1959-60,* India, 1960

142. ——————, "Increasing Agricultural Production in Early Stages in Economic Development," Unpublished paper presented at the Centre for Agricultural and Economic Adjustment Seminar at Ames, Iowa, February 1962, pp. 20-3

143. METZLER, W. H. and CHARLTON, J. L., "Employment and Underemployment in Rural People in the Ozarks," *Arkansas Agricultural Experimentation Station Bulletin,* Vol. DCIV, 1958

144. MOORE, W. E., *Industrialization and Labor,* New York, 1951

145. ————, *Economic Demography of Eastern and South-Eastern Europe,* Geneva, 1945

146. MORSE, NANCY AND WEISS, R. S., "The Function and Meaning of Work," in Sigmund Nosow and William H. Forum, ed., *Man, Work and Society,* New York, 1962

147. MUJUMDAR, N. A., "The Technique of Measuring Rural Unemployment," *Indian Journal of Agricultural Economics,* March 1954, Vol. IX, pp. 185-97

148. ——————, and Sovani, N. V., "On Unemployment and Development Planning-Conception Orientation," *Indian Economic Journal,* 1955, Vol. III, pp. 114-17

149. ——————, "Underemployment Micro and Macro and the Development Plan," *Indian Economic Journal,* 1955

150. ——————, "Concepts in Agricultural Employment," *Indian Journal of Agricultural Economics,* 1956, Vol. XI, pp. 46-8

151. ——————, "Economic Backwardness and Labor Force," *Indian Journal of Agricultural Economics,* 1957, Vol. XII, pp. 44-7.

152. ——————, "Some Problems of Underemployment," *Journal of the University of Bombay: Economics and Sociology Series,* 1957, Vol. XXVI. pp. 45-8

153. ——————"Some Aspects of Underemployment," *Indian Economic Journal,* 1957, Vol. V, pp. 1-18

154.——————, "Economic Development with Surplus Labour," *Indian Economic Journal,* 1960, Vol. VIII, pp. 284-314

155. ——————, "Full Employment for Rural Labour," *Indian Labour Journal,* 1960, pp. 569-75

156. ——————, *Some Problems of Underemployment,* Bombay, 1961

157. MUKERJI, P. K., "A Note on Agricultural Unemployment ʹand Level of Wages," *Indian Society of Agricultural Economics :* Seminar Series, 1956, pp. 68-75

158. ——————, *Economic Surveys in the Underdeveloped Countries,* London, 1959

159. NAKAGIMA, C., "Latent Unemployment and Agriculture of Peasantry,"

Osaka Economic Papers, 1955, Vol. IV, pp. 29-40

160. NANAVATI, M. B. and ANJARIA, J. J., *The Indian Rural Problems*, Bombay, 1960

161. NATIONAL COUNCIL OF APPLIED ECONOMIC RESEARCH, *Techno-Economic Survey of Punjab 1962*, New Delhi

162. NAVARRETE, ALFREDO and NAVARRETE, IFIGENIA M. DE, "Underemployment in Underdeveloped Countries," *International Economic Papers*, 1958, Vol. III, pp. 235-9

163. NEALE, WALTER C., *Economic Change in Rural India*, 1962

164. NURKSE, RAGNAR, *Problems of Capital Formation in Underdeveloped Countries*, Oxford, 1953

165. —————, "Excess Population and Capital Formation," *Malayan Economic Review*, October 1957, Vol. LXXI, pp. 188-204

166. —————, "Epilogue : The Quest for a Stabilization Policy in Primary Producing Countries," *Kyklos*, 1958, Vol. XI, pp. 261-2

167. *Ibid.*

168. OHATA. E.. *Full Employment and Latent Unemployment*. Tokyo. 1955

169. OHKAWA, KAZUSHI, "Economic Growth and Agriculture with Special Reference to the Productivity-Employment Problem," *Annals of Hitotsubashi Academy*, 1956, Vol. VII, pp. 46-59

170. OHKAWA, I., *Economic Analysis of Agriculture*, Tokyo, 1955

171. ORLANDO, G., "Unemployment and Underemployment in Agriculture," *Indian Journal of Agricultural Economics*, 1955, Vol. X, pp. 9-26

172. —————, "Investigation and Seasonality of Farm Work and Annual Employment of the Workers," *Review of Economics and Agriculture*, 1953, Vol. VIII, pp. 247-61

173. OSHIMA, HARRY T., "Underemployment in Backward Economies—An Empirical Comment," *The Journal of Political Economy*, June 1958, Vol. LXVI, pp. 259-64

174. —————, "The Ranis-Fei Model of Economic Development," *American Economic Review*, June 1963, pp. 448-52

175. OUCHI, T., *Total Estimate and Economic Importance of Population Surpluses in Agriculture*, Tokyo, 1955

176. PANDE, J. K., "Measurement of Rural Underemployment in Uttar Pradesh," *Indian Journal of Agricultural Economics*, 1954, Vol. IX, pp. 170-5

177. —————, "Pattern of Agricultural Labour in Uttar Pradesh," *Indian Journal of Agricultural Economics*, 1957, Vol. XII, pp. 77-83

178. PARK, R. E., *Race and Culture*, Chicago, 1950

179. PANNIKAR, K. S. L., "Some Problems of Measurement of Unemployment in a Semi-agricultural Village," *Indian Journal of Agricultural Economics*, 1954, Vol. IX, pp. 193-7

180. PARTHASARTHY, G., *Underemployment and Indian Agriculture*. Unpublished doctoral dissertation, University of Wisconsin, 1957

181.   —————, "Size of Farm Holdings and the Year-round Worker," *Journal of Gokhale Institute of Politics and Economics*, 1959, Vol. I, pp. 70-81

182.   —————, "Measurement of Employment, Unemployment and Underemployment in Rural Areas," *Papers read at Seminar on Concepts and Measurement of Unemployment*, The Institute of Economic Growth, Delhi, 1961

183.   PATEL, R. K., *The Nature and Extent of Underemployment of the Self-employed Cultivators*, Unpublished doctoral dissertation, University of Bombay, 1962

184.   PATEL, S. J., *Agricultural Labourers in India and Pakistan*, Bombay, 1952

185.   PATNAIK, S. R., "Employment and Potential of the Cottage and Small Scale Industries in India," *Indian Vikram University*, 1957, Vol. I, pp. 57-69

186.   PEPELASIS, ADAM A. and YOTOPOULOS, PAN A., *Surplus Labor in Greek Agriculture*, Center of Economic Research, Athens, Greece, 1962

187.   PEPELASIS, ADAM A., *Labor Shortages in Greek Agriculture*, 1963-1973, Athens, 1963

188.   PIGOU, A. C., *Industrial Fluctuations*, London, 1915

189.   POHERILLE, M., "Development and Rural Overpopulation: Some Lessons from Polish Experience, *International Labor Review*, March 1964

190.   PREST, A. R., *War Economics of Primary Producing Countries*, Cambridge, 1948

191.   PUERTO RICO, Department of Labor, *Results of Tests on Measuring Underemployment in Puerto Rico*, June-July 1952, San Juan, 1953

192.   PUERTO RICO, BUREAU OF LABOR STATISTICS, *Results of Tests on Measuring Underemployment in Puerto Rico*, June-July 1952

193.   PUNEKAR, S. D., "Labour Problems of India—A case study in Under-development," *India Labour Gazette*, 1958, Vol. XVI, pp. 367-72

194.   PUNJAB, BOARD OF ECONOMIC INQUIRY, PUNJAB (INDIA), *Survey of Rural Unemployment in the Punjab*, October-December 1955, Chandigarh, 1960

195.   —————, *Farm Accounts in the Punjab* (India), 1961-1962, Chandigarh, 1963

196.   RAJ, K. N., "Employment and Unemployment in the Indian Economy : Problems of Classification, Measurement and Policy," *Economic Development and Cultural Change*, 1959, Vol. VII, pp. 258-78

197.   RAMGOPAL, "Rural Employment and Increasing Pressure on Land in Uttar Pradesh," *Rural India*, 1954, Vol. XVII, pp. 182-4

198.   RANIS, GUSTAV and FEI, JOHN C. H., "A Theory of Economic Development," *American Economic Review*, September 1961, Vol. IV, pp. 533-65

199.   —————, *Development of the Labor Surplus Economy—Theory and Policy*, Homewood, 1964

200.   RAO, G. U. SUBHA, "The Impact of Industrialization on Indian Society,"

Columbia Journal of International Affairs, 1950, Vol. IV, pp. 50-60

201. RAO, V. K. R. V., "Full Employment and Economic Development," *Indian Economic Review*, August 1952

202. RAUP, PHILLIP M., "Economic Aspects of Population Decline in Rural Communities" in Iowa State University Press, ed. *Labor Mobility and Population*, Iowa, 1961

203. ————, "The Contribution of Land Reform to Agricultural Development: An Analytical Framework," *Economic Development and Cultural Change*, October 1963, Vol. XII, pp. 1-21

204. RICARDO, DAVID, *Principles of Political Economy and Taxation*, 1871

205. RISTIMAKI, TOINI, "Use of Manpower on Dwarf Farm," *Finnish Rural Labor Force Studies*, 1955, Vol. IV

206. RITTENHOUSE, IRMA, " Underemployment" in *Studies in Unemployment*, Joint Economic Committee U. S. Senate, Washington, D. C. 1960

207. ROBINSON, JOAN, "Disguised Unemployment," *Economic Journal*, June 1936, Vol. XXXXVI, pp. 225-37

208. ————, *Essays in the Theory of Employment*, London, 1947

209. ROSENSTEIN-RODAN, P. N., "The Role of Income Distribution in Development Program," *Rivista Internazionale di Scienze Economiche e Commerciali*, May 1965, Vol. XII, pp. 454-65.

210. ————, "Problems of Industrialization of Eastern and South-Eastern Europe," *Economic Journal*, June-September 1943, Vol. LIII, pp. 202-11

211. ————, "Disguised Unemployment and Underdevelopment in Agriculture," *Monthly Bulletin of Agricultural Economics and Statistics*, July-August 1957, Vol. VI, pp. 1-7

212. ROSSI, D. DE MEDELANA, "Unemployment in Agriculture, its Causes and Possible Remedies," *Rass dell Agricultural Atlas*, 1951, Vol. VI, pp. 7-9

213. ROTTENBERG, S., "The Immobility of Labor in Underdeveloped Areas," *South African Journal of Economics*, December 1951, Vol. XIX, pp. 404-8

214. ————, "Labor Force Measurement in a Pre-industrial Economy," *Southern Economic Journal*, 1951, Vol. XVIII, pp. 219-24

215. ————, "Income and Leisure in an Underdeveloped Economy," *Journal of Political Economy*, April 1952, Vol. LX, pp. 95-101

216. ROYAL INSTITUTE OF INTERNATIONAL AFFAIRS, *Unemployment—An International Problem*, London, 1935

217. ————, *Excess Population in Eastern and South Eastern Europe*, London, 1943

218. SARKAR, N. K., "A Method of Estimating Surplus Labor in Peasant Agriculture in Over-populated Underdeveloped Countries, *Journal of Royal Statistical Society: Serial A (General)* 1957, Vol. CXX, pp. 209-14

219. SAYIGH, Y. A., "Underemployment—Concept and Measurement, *Middle East Economic Papers*, 1956, Vol. III, pp. 127-42

220. SCHILLER, OTTO, "Cooperative Farms," *Indian Journal of Agricultural Economics*, October-December 1956

221. SCHULTZ, THEODORE W., "Latin-American Economic Policy Lessons," *American Economic Review*, May 1956, Vol. XXXXIV, pp. 425-32

222. —————, "Role of Government in Promoting Economic Growth," in Leonard D. White ed., *The State of the Social Sciences*, 1956

223. —————*The Economic Test in Latin America*, State School of Industrial and Labor Relations, Cornell University, Bulletin XXXV, August 1956

224. —————, *Transforming Traditional Agriculture*, Chicago, 1964

225. SEN, A. K., "Unemployment, Relative Prices and the Saving Potential," *Indian Economic Review*, August 1957, Vol. IV, pp. 56-63

226. —————, *Choice of Technique—An Aspect of the Theory of Planned Economic Development*, Oxford, 1962

227. SHANNON, LYLE W., "Occupational and Residential Adjustment of Rural Migrants," in Iowa State University Press ed., *Labor Mobility and Population in Agriculture*

228. SHASTRI, C. P., "Labor Utilization in Indian Farming," *Journal of Farm Economics* 1957, Vol. XXXIX, pp. 759-69

229. SHIVALKAR, R. S., "Techniques of Measuring Rural Underdevelopment," *Indian Journal of Agricultural Economics*, 1954, Vol. IX, pp. 155-61

230. SHUKLA, D. K., "The Problem of Employment and Economic Development of Underdeveloped Countries," *Journal Maharaja Sayajirao University of Baroda*, 1954, Vol. III, pp. 59-85

231. SHUMAN, C. B., "The Man with a Hoe," *Nation's Agriculture*, 1950, Vol. III

232. SIDGWICK, HENRY, *Principles of Political Economy*, 1883

233. SIMEY, T. S., *Welfare and Planning in West Indies*, London, 1946

234. SINGH, B., "An Employment Approach to the Third Five Year Plan," *Indian Labour Journal*, 1960, pp. 565-9

235. SINGH, TARLOK, *Progress and Social Change—A Study in Economic Reorganization of Indian Rural Society*, London, 1945

236. SINGH, V. B., "Disguised Unemployment or Underemployment?" *Indian Journal of Labour Economics*, 1958, Vol. I

237. SOM, R. K., and Bhattacharyya, G, C., "Type-Study on Peak Period in Harvesting Aman Paddy," *Sankhya*, 1960, Vol. XXII, pp. 131-42

238. SOVANI, N. V., "Underemployment, Micro-Macro and Development Planning," *Indian Economic Journal*, April 1955, Vol. II, pp. 301-10

239. —————, "Underemployment, Removable Surplus and the Saving Fund," *Artha Vijnana*, March 1959, Vol. I, pp. 17-29

240. SPENGLER, J. J., "Economic Factors in the Development of Densely Settled Areas," *Proceedings of the American Philosophical Society*, 1951, Vol. LXXXXV, pp. 21-53

241. SRINIVASAN, M., "Techniques of Measuring Rural Unemployment," *Indian Journal of Agricultural Economics*, March, 1954, Vol, IX, pp. 175-81

242. SUBRAMANIAN, N. R. R., "Agricultural Unemployment and Level of Agricultural Wages," *Indian Society of Agricultural Economic Seminar Series*, 1956, pp. 109-14

243. SURIYAKUMARAN, C., *The Economics with special reference to India and Ceylon*

244. SURYANARAYANAN, K. S., "Resource Returns in Telengana Farms—A Production Function Study," *Indian Journal of Agricultural Economics*, 1958 pp. 20-6

245. TAUHNER, C., *Utilization of Human Resources in Agriculture. Modernization Programs in Relation to Human Resources and Population Problems*, Milbank Memorial Fund, New York, 1950

246. TAYLOR, M. C., "A Note on Underemployment in Agriculture," *Journal of Farm Economics*, 1951, Vol. XXXIII, pp. 140-3

247. TELANG, M. A., "Technique of Measuring Rural Unemployment," *Indian Journal of Agricultural Economics*, March 1954, Vol. IX, pp. 150-4

248. TEWARI, S. G., "An Approach to the Measurement of Unemployment in India," *Indian Journal of Labour Economics*, 1959, Vol. I, pp. 477-82

249. THAKER, L. N., "Technique of Measuring Agricultural Unemployment," *Indian Journal of Agricultural Economics*, March 1954, Vol. IX, pp. 181-5

250. THEODORSON, G. A., "Acceptance of Industrialization and its Attendant Consequences for the Social Patterns of Non-Western Societies," *American Social Review*, 1953. Vol. XVIII, pp. 477-84

251. THURNER, D., "Agricultural Manpower in India," *Economic Weekly*, 1957, Vol. IX, pp. 1443-9

252. TINTNER, G. and BROWNLEE O. H., "Production Functions Derived from Farm Records," *Journal of Farm Economics*, 1944, Vol. XXVI, pp. 566-71

253. TREMELLONI, ROBERT, "The Parliamentary Inquiry into Unemployment in Italy," *International Labor Review*, September 1953, Vol. LXVIII, pp. 256-78

254. TSCHIYA, KEIZO, "Production Function in Japanese Agriculture," *Records of Research in the Faculty of Agriculture University of Tokyo*, March 1956, Vol. V, pp. 28-9

255. TSURU, SHIGETO, "Employment in Japan-Problems and Prospects," Far Eastern Survey, July 1957, reprinted in his *Essays in Japanese Economy* 1958

256. ——————, *Essays on Japanese Economy*, Tokyo, 1958

257. UMEMURA, M., *The Family Undertaking and the Labor Market*, Tokyo 1954

258. ——————, "Measurement of Disguised Unemployment in Punjab Agriculture," *Canadian Journal of Economics and Political Science*, November 1967, Vol. XXXIII, pp. 590-6

259. UPPAL, J. S., "Work Habits and Disguised Unemployment in an Underdeveloped Economy—A Theoretical Analysis," *Oxford Economic Papers*, November 1969, Vol. XXI, No. 3, pp. 387-94

260. UNITED NATIONS, DEPARTMENT OF ECONOMIC AFFAIRS, *Measures for the*

Economic Development of Underdeveloped Countries, New York, May 1951

261. ——————, "Disguised Unemployment and Forms of Business Organization in an Underdeveloped Economy," *Economia Internazionale*, Vol. XXIII, No. 1, 1970, pp. 68-73

262. VAKIL, C. N. and BRAHMANAND, *Planning for an Expanding Economy*, Bombay, 1956

263. VINER JACOB, "Some Reflections on the Concept of Disguised Unemployment," *Indian Journal of Economics*, July 1957, Vol. XXXVIII, pp. 17-23

264. VRIES, E., "Labor Standards and Wages In Agriculture in Underdeveloped Countries," *Journal of Farm Economics*, 1956, Vol. XXXVIII, pp. 540-2

265. WARRINER, DOREEN, *Economics of Peasant Farming*, Oxford 1939

266. —————— *Land and Poverty in the Middle East*, New York 1948

267. ——————*Land Reforms and Economic Development*, 50th Anniversary Commemoration Lectures, National Bank of Egypt, Cairo, 1955

268. WIJENAIKE, E. M., "The Problem of Underemployment in Ceylon," *Ceylon Labour Gazette*, 1952, Vol. III, pp. 3-15

269. WILCOX, W. W. and Hendrix, W. F., "Underemployment of Rural Families," in *Contemporary Readings in Agricultural Economics*, New York, 1955

270. WISE, T. F., "Methods of Using Surplus Population," *Pakistan Economic Journal*, March 1956, Vol. VI, pp. 97-103

271. WONNACOTT, PAUL, "Disguised Unemployment and Overt Unemployment in Underdeveloped Countries," *Quarterly Journal of Economics*, May 1962, Vol. LXXVI, pp. 279-97

272. YAKSHKIN, D., "Radical Changes in Agricultural Labor Conditions," *Indian Journal of Agricultural Economics*, 1959, Vol. XIV, pp. 45-7

273. YAMANKA, A., *Concepts of Latent Unemployment*, Tokyo, 1954

274. YAMANAKA, TOKUTARO, "On Latent Unemployment—An Interpretation as an Economic Problem," *The Annals of the Hitotsubashi Academy*, April 1956, Vol. VI, pp. 1-17

275. YATES, P. LAMARTINE AND WARRINER, DOREEN, *Food and Farming in Post-War Europe*, London, 1943

INDEX